KRUPS

The Encyclopedia of

Coffee and Espresso

From beans to brew

A Complete Guide For The Home Preparation of Filter Drip Coffee, Espresso, Cappuccino & Caffè Latte

Krups North America, Inc.
7 Reuten Drive
Closter, NJ 07624

INTRODUCTION

Welcome to the World of Krups

In over 100 countries throughout the world the name Krups is synonymous with the highest quality coffee and espresso brewing systems. Robert Krups GmbH & Co. was founded in 1846 in Solingen, Germany, as a manufacturer of industrial scales and weighing machines. Krups North America was established in the United States in 1976 and pioneered automatic filter drip coffee makers and espresso/cappuccino machines for the home.

Celebrating our 150th year, Krups is positioning itself for the year 2000. Our European tradition of the finest quality coffee equipment will continue with product innovation, advanced technology and sleek Euro-styling to complement any home decor.

The Krups dedication to coffee goes beyond the production of equipment. We passionately feel responsible for the pleasure you experience from every cup of drip coffee, espresso, cappuccino and caffè latte that you enjoy at home. We know full well that the finest brewing equipment will not produce satisfactory results unless you understand the basics to properly prepare your coffee.

The Krups Encyclopedia of Coffee and Espresso is designed to unravel the mysteries and provide the basics for both filter drip coffee and espresso brewing methods, regardless of the brand or type of equipment that you own or contemplate purchasing.

TABLE OF CONTENTS

TABLE OF CONTENTS

IMPORTANT NOTICE

The information in this book is not intended to supersede the information contained in the instruction manuals supplied by manufacturers of drip coffee, espresso and cappuccino equipment.

Since each machine has its own operating specifications and safety features, the publisher and distributor disclaim all liability incurred in connection with the generalized information contained in this book. The publisher and distributor make no warranty of any kind, expressed or implied, with regard to the instructions and suggestions contained in this book.

Please carefully read the operational instructions and safety notices supplied with your machine.

CHAPTER ONE

ALL
ABOUT
COFFEE

ALL ABOUT COFFEE

The discovery and cultivation of coffee reads like a thrilling, mystifying Cold War spy novel, except that the events have taken place over centuries instead of decades. Coffee affects the lives of millions and the economies of many nations. The history of coffee is spiced with international intrigue, political deception and romance, all buried in fact and fable.

Coffee is the second largest commodity traded in the world, second only to oil. Coffee grows in more than 50 countries throughout the world, and the economies of many coffee-producing countries are completely dependent on this commodity.

A Brief History

The best known legend surrounding the discovery of coffee concerns Kaldi, an Ethiopian goat herder who one day found his goats acting like kids. They had been eating red berries from a shiny, dark-leafed shrub growing on the hillside. Kaldi tried the berries and pranced with the goats. An abbot watched this activity and gave some of the berries to neighboring monks, who prayed all night without falling asleep.

More likely, coffee was first noticed by wandering tribesmen known to have eaten the berries crushed to a pulp, mixed with animal fats, and rolled into balls of food. Later the green beans were steeped in water as a broth, when the Arabs discovered how to boil water around the year 1000 A.D. By the end of the 14th century roasting and grinding the beans became popular in Arabia.

The Arabs first used coffee as a medicine, and the medicinal aspect remained associated with coffee for centuries. It was used as a beverage during religious and meditation ceremonies to fight fatigue. The Koran forbids drinking alcoholic beverages, which increased the popularity of coffee. The word coffee stems from the Arab word "qahwa" meaning a drink made from plants, and in Europe coffee was often called the "wine of Arabia".

The Arabs sought to control the export of coffee by only allowing parched or boiled beans that would not germinate to be exported. The traditional pilgrimages to Mecca ended this monopoly when some of the pilgrims carried the cherished beans back to their homelands. Eventually coffee spread to the Middle East and on to Persia, Egypt, North Africa and Turkey.

Being great travelers, Venetians may have been the first Europeans to acquire coffee. Medicinal qualities were still being stressed in 1580 when coffee was brought from Egypt. Some Italian wine growers became alarmed at possible competition, and they petitioned the Pope to ban coffee. But, when the Pope tasted it, he enjoyed it so much he gave it his blessing.

The Dutch recognized the value of coffee and cultivated it in the East Indies in 1699, most notably the island of Java. In an effort to impress Louis XIV of France, the Dutch presented him with a valuable coffee tree in 1715, which was protected under tight security in a special greenhouse at the palace of Versailles. The French cultivated coffee in the West Indies, after a perilous journey from France to Martinique in 1723 where only one of three coffee trees survived. After a brief romantic liaison, another coffee tree was spirited to Brazil, which became the largest coffee-producing country in the world.

By the 17th century, the seeds of one legendary tree became a worldwide passion. Records show coffee was first served in 1668 in New York as a beverage brewed from beans and sweetened with honey. Soon all of the colonies had founded coffeehouses. John Adams and Paul Revere allegedly plotted the American Revolution at the Green Dragon Coffee House in Boston.

For hundreds of years, coffee supplies were abundant, but eventually coffee consumption all over the world was beginning to deplete the available supplies. After World War II, the quality of coffee in the United States declined and, by the 1960's, less expensive robusta beans were used in high-volume commercial blends. The electric coffee percolator popular at that time further deteriorated the coffee flavor .

An example of the volatility of coffee as an important worldwide commodity is the disaster that struck in 1975, when a sudden frost in Brazil destroyed millions of trees. Shortly after, civil war in Angola cut their harvest; floods in Colombia destroyed trees; an earthquake in Guatemala depleted the crop, and many other Central American countries were forced to deal with the disease called coffee rust. Coffee prices soared.

In spite of higher prices, coffee sales remained reasonably stable. The higher quality "gourmet" coffee market began to spread throughout North America in the late 1970's. A significant development in the industry was the tremendous growth in the number of specialty coffee roasters and retailers during the 1980's that continues today. This phenomenon is stimulated by improvements in brewing equipment and the more recent interest in specialty coffee.

Cultivating Coffee

Coffee is cultivated between the Tropic of Cancer and the Tropic of Capricorn, where there is little seasonal change in climate. Frost is the coffee tree's worst enemy, and shade trees are often planted to protect the valuable crop from sudden changes in temperature.

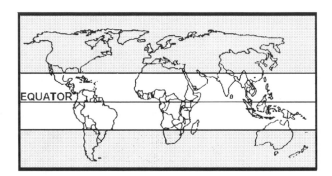

Arabica:

The Coffea arabica tree is very sensitive and requires an almost perfect balance of sunshine, shade and rain. The differences in flavor are caused by variations in soil, climate, humidity and the amount of annual rain fall. The tree grows naturally to a height of 20 feet, but is usually cultivated at six to ten feet to make harvesting easier and help increase the yield. Maximum productivity occurs after ten years, and begins to decrease after 20 years.

Coffea arabica is referred to as "high grown" coffee because the arabica tree only grows at elevations above 3,000 feet, producing less than two pounds of coffee per tree within three to five years of planting. An estimated 2,000 arabica cherries yield one pound of beans.

Robusta:

Coffea canephora (robusta) was discovered growing wild in the Belgian Congo, now Zaire. Grown at lower altitudes, from sea level to 2,000 feet, as its name implies, Robusta is cultivated for the hardiness and fertility of the tree. Each tree produces enough fruit for four pounds of coffee within two to three years of planting. Robusta beans are smaller and rounder with twice the caffeine of arabicas.

There is no comparison in flavor between arabica and robusta beans. Robusta can impart more body in the cup, if carefully blended with arabicas, but robusta beans tend to have a bitter flavor due to the higher caffeine content. Robusta accounts for 75% of world coffee traded, mainly used for high-volume commercial blends and soluble (instant) coffee.

Harvesting Coffee

The coffee tree has dark green, leathery, oblong leaves with small, white, fragrant flowers. The clustered fruit of the tree turns green from six to nine months after flowering and then ripens to a red berry that resembles a cherry (coffee berries are called cherries).

Growing coffee is a very labor-intensive industry, and few products require as much human handling. The cherries must be picked quickly, as they ripen over a period of days. The cherries are often picked by hand as they ripen, and pickers return to a tree five or six times. One branch of the tree may have white flowers, green (unripe) berries, and ripened fruit cherries all at one time during the short ripening period.

Hand-picking coffee is the preferred method and obviously more expensive. Machines used to strip the coffee tree of ripened berries cannot discriminate between green and red berries, or even flowers and branch bits.

Processing The Bean

The actual red berry contains two seeds with flat sides facing each other. These are the coffee beans. The outside skin of the berry contains a fruit pulp, and each bean is wrapped in an outer parchment and an inner silver skin. Occasionally, nature provides a single round bean, called a peaberry, instead of two flat beans per cherry.

A delicate stage is processing the coffee cherries to remove the outer husk and reveal the beans. The cherries are processed in one of two methods, or a combination of both: a wet method (washed) before the cherries have dried, or a dry/natural method (unwashed) where the cherries are dried naturally. The process chosen often depends on the availability of water in the coffee-producing region. Regardless of the method (wet or dry), the care taken in processing the cherries has a profound impact on the quality and final cost of the beans.

SKIN
PULP
PARCHMENT
SILVER SKIN
COFFEE BEAN

The wet, or washed, method is a complex process that removes the outer layers of the cherry by soaking the cherries in tanks for 12 to 24 hours. The delicate fermentation process takes place before the beans have dried. The beans are thoroughly washed, drained, and dried in the sun or by mechanical driers that provide a current of hot air.

Hulling or milling machines remove the last protective parchment and silver skin. The wet or washed process is more expensive, and is said to be superior in providing a more consistent flavor.

The natural, or dry, method is an older process where the cherries are spread in the sun to dry naturally in one to three weeks and raked several times a day to protect them from moisture. Fermentation takes place while the beans are drying, and the outer layers are allowed to shrivel around the beans. The dried hull is removed by milling machines.

Unless the cherries are hand-picked, the dry method is considered inferior because it also processes cherries that have not fully ripened, providing a more variable flavor. However, some of the world's most interesting varietals are dry processed beans.

Grading The Beans

Grading is the step in the process that establishes the value of the green beans eventually sold to roasters. The beans are sorted for size by hand, or by a shaking machine. Technology has introduced machines with an electronic eye that sort the beans by size and color.

The grade of a particular bean will vary by region, and no two crops are identical. By sizing and grading the beans, defects are discovered. As an example, broken beans are considered a defect because they roast darker and can negatively affect an entire batch of roast.

After grading the beans are bagged for trading and export to roasters. Straight coffees in the green bean stage are called varietals, and will keep for several years. It is the roasting process that brings out the subtle characteristics of each varietal.

The Roast

The roasting process forces moisture out of the bean and brings volatile oils closer to the surface of the bean. The essence of the coffee flavor is in these delicate oils. As the temperature in the roaster increases (up to 450°F) the roast darkens, and a dark roast can have less caffeine than a lighter roast.

As the high heat of the roaster forces moisture out of the bean, the bean expands but the weight diminishes. One pound of a light roast will be less volume that one pound of a dark espresso roast.

There is no precise standardized terminology used to describe the coffee roast. Viennese, Italian, French and American are not the origin of the bean but instead refer to the degree of roasting (length of time and temperature) and that depends on the standards of the roaster.

In some regions, a French roast would indicate the darkest possible roast, whereas in other regions an Italian roast may indicate the darkest roast. The roasting process determines the character of any coffee flavor, and roastmasters take great pride in their art. The degree of roast is totally dependent on the roaster, but the preferred roast is still a matter of personal taste.

The Blend

Blending provides the balance between the strength of one varietal and the delicate flavor of another. Because each varietal has a different size and weight, the beans react differently in the roasting process. Each blend has its own taste characteristics based on the origin of the beans and how they are roasted.

The blending of straight coffees provides the final nuance of flavor, and the roastmaster enhances the subtle characteristics of each group in the roasting process.

Anywhere from three to ten straight coffees are blended, either by the roaster or a specialty coffee retailer. The blend and roast of the whole bean are a matter of personal taste.

There are hundreds of different blends developed by coffee roasters and specialty coffee retailers. Discuss the many different blends with your local roaster or retailer, and experiment freely in selecting a blend and roast. Just make sure the beans are fresh and ground to the right consistency for your coffee brewing equipment.

Purchasing Coffee

The quality of your coffee in the cup will only be as good as the freshness and quality of the beans you buy. When purchasing coffee, important considerations are where the green beans originated, the degree or length of time they were roasted, when they were roasted, and the blend.

How often a retailer's whole bean stock is turned will be an indication of the freshness of the roast. Whole beans retain their flavor and freshness for only two to four weeks after roasting, depending upon how the beans are stored.

When purchasing fresh ground coffee from a specialty coffee retailer, consider buying smaller quantities more often, which will also give you an opportunity to experiment with their "house" blends. Whole beans from a specialty coffee retailer are usually fresher than beans sold at a supermarket. Specialty coffee retailers have the knowledge and interest in your satisfaction that make it well worth the effort to locate them.

If you do not own a grinder, when purchasing pre-ground coffee keep in mind that once the beans are ground, more surface area is exposed to air. Unprotected pre-ground coffee will lose some of its flavor within two to three hours after grinding. You can delay the flavor evaporation process by properly storing your pre-ground and whole bean coffee.

Storing Coffee

The roasting process forces moisture out of the bean and brings the delicate oils closer to the surface of the bean. Fresh roasted whole beans begin to dissipate flavor rapidly, and pre-ground coffee begins to dissipate flavor immediately. Oxygen, light and humidity are the culprits that zap the flavor from freshly roasted (and ground) coffee.

Buy a small air-tight container especially for your coffee, small enough for the amount of coffee leaving the least amount of oxygen in the sealed container. An air-tight glass or ceramic container with a rubber seal is recommended, kept in a cool, dry and dark area.

The best place to store coffee is a controversial issue among professionals. Some recommend freezer storage in a sealed container to prolong the freshness of whole beans. Others believe the moisture generated by the refrigerator or freezer deteriorates the flavor.

Whole beans or pre-ground coffee stored in the refrigerator can deteriorate quickly, since moisture and odors will find their way even through a sealed container by condensation. In addition, darker roasted, oilier beans that are refrigerated tend to gum up in a burr grinder.

Consider buying only the amount of coffee you plan to use within two weeks for the freshest flavor. If the quantity of whole beans is more than you plan to use in 30 days, the freshness may be prolonged by keeping the beans in freezer storage. If you must freeze your excess coffee beans, try to remove as much air from the container as possible, and hope for the best. Take a look inside a frozen vegetable package, and you will see the crystallized condensation inside the package even through the package was sealed.

Because whole beans retain their freshness longer than pre-ground coffee, you may eventually determine the cost of a burr grinder is worth the investment, since you can adjust the grind to suit your drip coffee and pump-driven espresso equipment.

Coffee Packaging

Plain Brown Bag

Most retailers package beans or pre-ground coffee in a plain brown or decorated bag. This bag affords no protection against humidity, oxygen or moisture, all of which are enemies of freshly roasted coffee. Your purchase should be immediately transferred to an air-tight container, the right size for the amount of coffee you consume within two weeks.

Vacuum Packed Can

Because freshly roasted and freshly ground coffee release carbon dioxide gas, the coffee must be degassed (exposed to air) before it is vacuum packed. If coffee were not degassed before vacuum packaging in a can, the pressure would cause the can to burst. In the case of vacuum packed beans, the degassing process can take up to several days (for ground coffee up to several hours) which, unfortunately, dissipates some of the volatile oils that contain the desirable coffee flavor.

Most pre-ground vacuum packed coffee in cans is a coarse grind for drip coffee or non-pump steam pressure systems, so be sure to read the description to determine the right grind for your brewing equipment.

One-Way Valve Bags

This type of packaging is a great improvement over vacuum packed cans, since it allows the carbon dioxide gas to escape through a one-way valve without allowing oxygen to enter the package and dissipate flavor. The one-way valve system allows freshly roasted coffee to be packaged immediately and extends the shelf-life of the coffee up to three months or more.

Once the package is opened, there is no protection to prolong the freshness of the beans or the pre-ground coffee, and the coffee should be immediately transferred to an air-tight container for storage.

Vacuum (Brick) Pack

A relatively new innovation, this type of packaging makes it possible to pack freshly roasted beans and pre-ground coffee in a heavy plastic film, shaped like a brick and almost as hard. This type of package is usually sold in 250 gram or 500 gram packs with a shelf-life of six to eight months. Once the brick pack is opened, the staling process begins immediately and proper storage is highly recommended.

Capsules

Another relatively recent system, the capsule concept adds convenience as well as extended shelf-life. Air-tight capsules contain a pre-measured, fine grind espresso coffee designed to fit into the filter holder coffee basket of specially-designed pump-driven espresso machines, such as the Krups Nespresso system.

Decaffeinated Coffee

Each individual metabolizes caffeine differently, and decaffeinated coffee can be a good alternative for those adversely affected by caffeine.

Different coffee varietals have different caffeine contents. Specialty coffee with a high content of arabica beans has less than half the caffeine of robustas often used in commercial blends. Darker roasts tend to have less caffeine that lighter roasts, due to the longer roasting temperature that reduces the caffeine content.

For a coffee to be labeled "decaffeinated", at least 97% of the caffeine must be removed. It is a challenge to remove the caffeine from the beans and not remove the coffee flavor. The direct and indirect use of solvents in decaffeinating coffee have proponents and critics for every method. Caffeine is a water-soluble alkaloid and, in its pure form, caffeine is a bitter, white powder used as a stimulant and diuretic.

By soaking the green coffee beans in water, solvents are used to separate the caffeine from the water. The water with the coffee flavor is added back to the beans with at least 97% of the caffeine removed.

More recent water-processes use charcoal or carbon filters, instead of solvents, to separate the caffeine from the water. Technology continues to improve the process, which now includes "chemical-free" and "naturally decaffeinated" methods.

It is estimated that 25% of coffee sales today are of decaffeinated coffee, and as the market grows the quality of decaf coffee improves. The extra steps and handling involved in the decaffeination process are costly. Also, decaffeinated beans tend to roast darker and are more difficult to roast. Therefore, decaf coffee is more expensive, but a boon for those affected by caffeine.

Organic Coffee

Organic beans are certified by U.S. government or independent agencies to be cultivated in areas free of pesticides and chemicals in the soil used to improve a coffee yield. Professionals continue to debate the organic issue, from questioning the certification process to claiming organic beans lack flavor. Organic coffees are growing in popularity among the health conscious and environmentally concerned, which results in a wider variety of organic coffees becoming available.

CHAPTER TWO

COFFEE GRINDERS AND THE GRIND

COFFEE GRINDERS

One of the most critical elements in fully extracting the rich coffee flavor is the consistency and uniformity of the ground coffee. You can invest in the most expensive equipment and the finest and freshest coffee but, unless the beans are ground to the proper consistency for your brewing method, the finished product may be disappointing.

Grinding breaks up the coffee beans into thousands of small particles, thereby increasing the surface area that comes in contact with the water. The consistency of the grind affects the amount of time water is in contact with the coffee. The correct grind is essential to extracting the delicate nuances of the coffee flavor developed in the roast and blend. There are two basic types of coffee grinders; a blade grinder and a burr grinder.

Blade Grinder

Electric blade grinders whirl two blades at high speed which chop the beans into small particles. Controlling the grind is based on activating the On/Off switch that starts and stops the whirling blades.

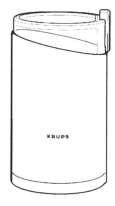

Use short pulses (several seconds) and a slight shake of the grinder to improve the consistency. Long exposure to the whirling blades can generate heat in the ground coffee that dissipates flavor. A circular bean hopper around the blades offers less control than an oval shape, because the beans collect in a circle around and underneath the blades. An oval shaped bean hopper moves the beans back toward the blades for additional grinding.

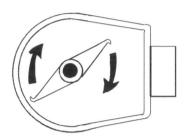

Blade grinders are not recommended for grinding espresso for a pump-driven system. For espresso, a consistent, fine grind is required. The whirling blades knock the coffee beans into both larger pieces as well as a part dust or powder. This powdery grind may clog the small perforations in the coffee basket of the espresso filter holder, completely restricting the flow of water through the espresso grind.

Blade grinders are relatively inexpensive and quite efficient for preparing a coarser grind for filter drip coffee and non-pump steam pressure espresso machines.

Hand Mill

Until the advent of electric grinders and pre-ground vacuum packed coffee, every household had a hand-operated burr grinder. Almost everyone's great- or great-great grandmother started the morning chores by placing a box grinder between her knees and turning the crank to prepare the morning's wake up brew. The sound and aroma of the coffee mill ritual started the day for generations of people througout the world.

The hand grinder is a manual version of the electric burr grinder and an extension of the grain mill and mortar and pestle. Whole beans are ground between two corrugated steel disks, or burrs, one stationary and the other rotating. The crank handle provides the control over the rotation and features an adjustment nut that sets the distance between the burrs to control the consistency of the grind.

A good quality hand burr grinder will provide a consistent, fine grind for espresso; however, the manual operation requires some patience.

Burr Grinders

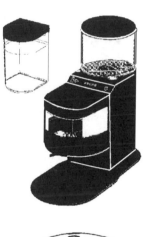

Electric burr grinders feature grinding adjustments from coarse to very fine. Opposing burrs shave the whole beans to a uniform grind by the chosen index setting or distance between the burrs. The top burr is stationary and the bottom burr rotates. Burr grinders minimize heat in the grinding process, and provide a more consistent grind.

Burr grinders for home use usually have a flat or slightly tapered set of corrugated burrs. More expensive or commercial versions of the burr grinder have a deeper taper or conical shape for an even more precise adjustment and grind.

Most burr grinders dispense ground coffee into a collection chamber, and ground coffee is spooned from the chamber into the coffee basket or espresso filter holder.

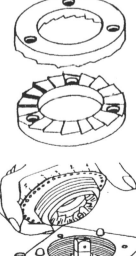

Some burr grinders feature an espresso doser with a lever that sweeps a pre-measured dose of the ground coffee directly into the espresso filter holder. One sweep of the lever doses roughly seven grams of coffee into the filter holder for a single serving, and two sweeps for a double serving.

A burr grinder will not only contribute to your enjoyment of espresso, but will also improve the flavor of your filter drip coffee. As an additional benefit, you may eventually save money since whole beans retain their flavor much longer than pre-ground coffee.

The Grind

A medium grind is coarser and has less surface area for longer filter drip brewing. A finer grind for espresso increases the surface area in contact with the water for brewing quickly under pressure.

There are two categories of grind consistency: a medium coarse grind for filter drip coffee and non-pump steam pressure machines; and a fine to extra-fine grind for pump-driven espresso machines. Within these two basic categories there are several consistency levels dictated by the brewing equipment and personal taste preferences.

Water follows the path of least resistance, either by gravity or especially water under pressure. If the grind is too coarse, the water will flow too quickly through the coffee basket with insufficient contact with the coffee. If the grind is too fine, the water cannot flow through the grind even under pressure.

Grinding beans may require a period of trial and error to fine-tune the consistency of the grind to your particular brewing method and equipment.

Whether you own your own grinder or purchase pre-ground coffee from a specialty coffee retailer, several basic rules apply.

Filter Drip Coffee Grind

A filter drip grind usually has a coarser texture. In a filter drip coffee system the heated water is seeped through the grind by gravity. Remember, the finer the grind, the more surface area comes into contact with the water for more flavor extraction.

If the grind is too fine, the water will not flow freely through the grind. It will take longer to brew the coffee, which can result in overextraction and a bitter taste. In addition, ground too finely, the grind may penetrate the paper or mesh filter and deliver some sediment into the carafe.

If the grind is too coarse, the water will flow too quickly through the grind, and not saturate the entire quantity of coffee in the paper or mesh filter. A grind too coarse for your drip coffee system can result in a weak brew that lacks the full coffee flavor.

The correct ratio of ground coffee to the quantity of water will also improve the brew. Use one full measuring spoon of coffee for every five ounces of water.

If you grind your own whole beans, only grind the amount you plan to use immediately, since ground coffee stales quickly and begins to lose much of the flavor and volatile oils.

The Espresso Grind

Within the espresso category there are two types of grind; a medium fine grind with a coarser texture for non-pump steam-pressure systems, and an extra-fine grind for pump-driven espresso machines.

A non-pump machine develops from 3 to 5 bar of encapsulated steam pressure, which is insufficient to force the heated water through a very fine grind. By comparison, a pump driven machine develops from 13 to 16 bar of pump pressure, which will penetrate a finer grind.

The right espresso grind provides the resistance to the water under pressure that is essential to extracting the heart of espresso flavor. The grind for a pump-driven espresso machine should feel gritty, like salt, when rubbed between your fingers.

However, you should not grind the coffee too fine, since a powder grind (with the consistency of flour) will keep the water from penetrating the powder grind even under pump pressure. If the grind is too fine, coffee may spurt from around the seal between the brew head and filter holder.

A very fine powder grind can also clog the small perforations in the filter holder coffee basket and completely restrict the flow of water. A powder grind is used mainly for preparing Turkish coffee where the grind is added to boiling water in a vessel and consumed with the brew.

Another variable is the quantity of coffee used and the pressure applied when tamping the coffee in the coffee basket. A more powerful machine develops greater pressure and will brew through a finer grind.

Grinder Maintenance

It is important to keep your coffee grinder clean. An oily coffee residue will accumulate on the grinding mechanism (blade or burr) that can turn rancid and contaminate the coffee flavor.

Blade Grinder Maintenance

Always unplug the unit before removing the grinder lid. With a stiff brush, loosen any coffee residue from around the blades and wipe the interior of the grinding chamber with a damp cloth.

Wipe the housing with a clean damp cloth, but do not immerse the grinder in water. Wash the grinder lid by hand in mild soapy water and rinse thoroughly to remove all soap residue.

Burr Grinder Maintenance

Wipe the housing with a damp cloth, but do not immerse the grinder in water. The bean hopper and collection chamber or doser should be washed frequently, by hand, in mild soapy water and rinsed thoroughly to remove all soap residue. The burrs should be cleaned periodically with a stiff brush to remove any oils and gummy coffee residue. Grinder brushes are now available from many speciality coffee retailers.

Eventually the burrs will become dull and need replacing, but this would be after more than five years of normal home use. In a commercial environment the grinder burrs are usually replaced after 600 pounds of coffee have been ground.

Many burr grinders "spit" ground coffee onto the counter top, but there does not seem to be any way to avoid ground coffee residue unless you step up to one of the more expensive commercial-type burr grinders with a gear reduction motor.

CHAPTER THREE

FILTER DRIP COFFEE MAKERS

History of Coffee Brewing Methods

The evolution of the filter drip coffee beverage we enjoy today began with a separation of the coffee grounds from the brewing water. How water is brought into contact with coffee, at what temperature, and how long water is in contact with the coffee are rituals that still vary throughout the world.

The first attempt at transforming coffee from an edible food to a beverage was based on immersing green unroasted beans in a pot of water. This extracted a very medicinal and unsavory brew by today's standards.

It was not until the 14th century that Arabs learned to roast coffee and pulverize the beans with a mortar and pestle. This open pot brewing method resembled Turkish coffee, still enjoyed today in several countries. In the Turkish tradition, coffee is brought to boil no less than three times in a small pot, called an ibrik. The fine coffee powder-like grind is consumed with the coffee, usually heavily sweetened with sugar and cardamom. Due to the gritty texture, Turkish coffee is an acquired taste.

The open pot boiling method prevailed for over 400 years, until the Europeans became feverishly involved in developing new brewing methods to improve the coffee flavor.

American pioneers moving West used the open pot brewing method, known as Cowboy Coffee. Ground coffee was added to an enameled coffee pot filled with water and brought to boiling over a campfire. Cold water or egg shells were added after the water boiled to settle the grounds.

One of the first major brewing improvements took place in France in 1819 with the development of the gravity filter drip coffee system, using a perforated metal filter to separate the grounds from the liquid. Quickly adopted by the Italians in Naples, this "flip-drip" pot is now referred to as the Neopolitan. Water is heated in one chamber and inverted or flipped over a coffee chamber. The water seeps through the metal coffee basket into a serving chamber, which is disconnected from the coffee chamber for serving.

The French refined the filter drip system, developing metal or porcelain filters that suspended the coffee over a vessel. Heated water was poured over the ground coffee at a temperature below boiling. Café filtre is still enjoyed today, with cloth, paper and mesh filters as an alternative to metal or porcelain.

The French also developed the press or plunger system, using a filter the same diameter as the open pot to plunge the ground coffee to the bottom of the carafe and separate the grounds from the brew. The French Press is still in use today.

An even more significant development that had a profound impact on American coffee drinking habits was the pumping percolator developed in France in 1827. Although this system was not universally accepted in Europe, the stove-top percolator later became the favored method of brewing coffee in North America.

In the 1950's an electric version of the stove-top percolator emerged and, until the late 1960's, Americans were quite content to overextract their coffee in the electric percolator. Although convenient, the percolator continually reintroduced the brewed coffee to the already saturated coffee grounds in the metal coffee basket. The wonderful aroma generated by the electric percolator meant the true coffee flavor was dissipating in the air.

Today both the boiling method and percolation are rarely used in North America. But only recently did we begin to recognize the flavor advantages of a more controlled brewing method that evolved from European systems.

In 1970 the automatic filter drip coffee system was introduced, and quickly became the accepted brewing method because of the improved flavor extraction.

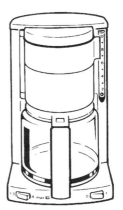

Automatic filter drip coffee makers in the '90's are extremely efficient and convenient, incorporating many innovative features, such as adjustable brewing cycles, water filtration systems and programmable timers for "wake-up" coffee.

Filter Drip Coffee Makers

Overview

After experimenting for centuries with different types of coffee brewing methods, the automatic filter drip coffee maker is by far the most efficient and convenient way to extract the rich flavor from ground coffee.

Although a variety of filter drip coffee makers are available, they are not all created equal in terms of performance and flavor extraction. Further research and development resulted in improvements from bare-boned filter drip systems to sophisticated machines that incorporate all the basic elements that produce a flavorful cup of coffee.

Some of the technical enhancements that should be considered when purchasing an automatic filter drip coffee maker are outlined below.

Deep Brew Technology

More sophisticated filter drip systems feature electronic control over the water temperature and brewing cycle. The water temperature is controlled between 197° and 205°F, and the water is pulsed through the ground coffee at precisely timed intervals. The pulses are measured to insure that the entire bed of coffee is saturated, until the coffee is at the peak of robust flavor.

Controlled Brewing Cycle

The brewing cycle is adjusted to compensate for the time the ground coffee is in contact with the water. Adjusting the extraction time controls the brewing cycle for three full-bodied cups of coffee from a ten-cup coffee maker.

Coffee Filter Holder

A cone-shape to the coffee filter holder is important in controlling the full extraction of the coffee flavor. A cone-shaped filter holder insures the full saturation and complete extraction of the rich coffee flavor. A basket-shaped filter holder spreads the ground coffee over a larger area.

Double-Walled Filter Holder

A double-walled filter holder prevents the loss of heat and aroma during the coffee brewing cycle. The outer wall reflects back the heat that otherwise escapes in the brewing process.

Water Filtration System

A more recent feature incorporated into the more sophisticated filter drip coffee systems, the charcoal water filter purifies the water by removing unwanted chlorine taste and odor. Because coffee is 98% water, the purity and quality of the water are an important element in the brewing process.

24-Hour Programmable Timer

If your body clock is tuned into a "wake-up" cup of coffee, this feature guarantees a quick start first thing in the morning. The timer is programmed to automatically begin the brewing cycle at a pre-determined time.

Stop 'N Serve

The Stop 'N Serve interupts the brewing cycle and allows the removal of the carafe to pour a first serving - the answer for those who clamor for a quick cup of coffee.

Aroma Savor Lid

This feature automatically seals the lid of the carafe after the brewing cycle is completed. When the last drop of coffee leaves the filter holder, it seals the opening within the lid of the carafe to reduce the evaporation of heat and flavor. The carafe becomes air-tight and protects the aroma and freshness of the coffee.

Automatic Shut-Off

The Auto Shut-Off feature automatically turns off the heating element, usually one hour after the brewing cycle is completed, to prevent the coffee from scalding and losing flavor. Some machines can be programmed to automatically shut off in one to five hour increments.

Thermostatically-Controlled Heating Plate

Maintains the heat of the coffee in the carafe at one of six intervals, for a serving temperature from 149° to 194°F.

Insulated Thermal Carafes

The double insulated thermal glass carafe keeps the coffee hot for up to five hours and seals in the flavor. Some automatic filter drip coffee makers brew directly into a thermal carafe.

STEP-BY-STEP GUIDE TO AUTOMATIC FILTER DRIP COFFEE MAKERS

IMPORTANT

The following guide is general in nature and not intended to supersede the instructions provided by the manufacturer of your machine. Please read your owner's manual carefully. Each machine has its own operating specifications and safety features. The name and location of switches and controls vary on each machine. Please refer to your factory instruction manual for the position and specific function of the controls related to your machine

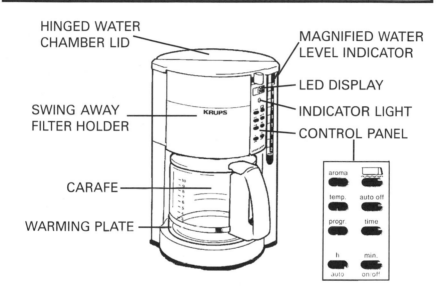

Automatic filter drip coffee makers are available in a wide variety of styles, ranging from the simple single switch On/Off maker to more sophisticated programmable systems. All automatic filter drip coffee makers have one thing in common, and that is a basic On/Off switch that triggers the coffee brewing cycle.

If you have a coffee maker with a variety of features, you can program the features in accordance with your personal preferences. Always refer to the instruction manual provided by the manufacturer of your particular machine.

Regardless of the type of machine you have, two factors are extremely important in brewing flavorful and robust drip coffee. The water must be cold and fresh, and the coffee must be fresh and ground to the right consistency for a filter drip coffee system.

Before connecting the appliance to an electrical outlet, be sure the Power Switch is in the "Off" position.

Open the hinged lid above the water chamber and pour in the desired quantity of water, as specified in your Owner's Manual and related to the number of servings you will brew. Most machines have a water level indicator that shows how much water is in the chamber.

The amount of freshly brewed coffee delivered after the brewing cycle is complete will always be slightly less than the amount of water added to the water chamber. This is due to the minimal absorption of water by the ground coffee. Therefore, add a little extra water to the desired number of servings.

The coffee filter holder holds the paper or mesh filter that contains the ground coffee. If your coffee filter holder is attached to the machine, open the Swing-Away Filter Holder. Some machines feature a release button to open the filter holder.

If your coffee filter holder is not connected to the machine, the filter holder and lid assembly rest on top of the carafe and can be removed as one unit.

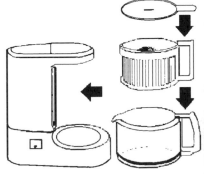

Insert a paper filter or mesh filter into the filter holder basket. Refer to your instruction manual for the style and size of paper or mesh filter for your particular machine.

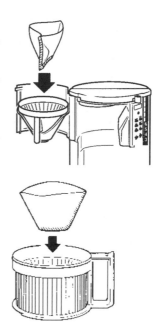

If a paper filter is used, be sure that the paper conforms to the outline of the filter holder and is not folded over, which would redirect the supply of water outside the filter and bypass the ground coffee.

Add ground coffee into the paper or mesh filter in the filter holder. It is suggested that you use one level measuring spoon of ground coffee for each cup of brewed coffee.

The measured amount of coffee in relation to the amount of water will determine the strength or weakness of the final brew. Adjust the amount of ground coffee in the filter and water in the chamber based on your own personal preference.

Replace the filter holder into the machine so that it is properly seated and locked in place.

Some machines feature only an "On/Off" switch, while others have a touch pad control for programming different functions.

If you have a filter drip coffee maker with a programmable timer, you should program these features prior to activating the Power Switch to "On".

Depress the Power Switch to the "On" position. An indicator light will illuminate to indicate the brewing cycle has begun.

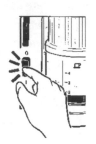

After a short delay, you should begin to see the brewed coffee dispensing into the coffee carafe.

When the brewing cycle is completed, the coffee temperature will be maintained at the proper drinking temperature by the thermostically-controlled warming plate beneath the carafe.

It is recommended that you not allow the coffee in the carafe to remain on the warming plate for an extended period of time, since coffee flavor dissipates very quickly at the warming plate temperature.

Some automatic filter drip coffee makers brew directly into a thermal carafe and do not have a warming plate.

It is suggested that you transfer coffee you do not intend to drink within 30 minutes into a thermal carafe to maintain the heat of the coffee for several hours without scalding or dissipating the flavor.

Turn the Power Switch "Off". Allow the machine to cool slightly before removing the filter from the filter holder to dispose of the coffee grounds.

KRUPS

FILTER DRIP COFFEE PRODUCT REVIEW

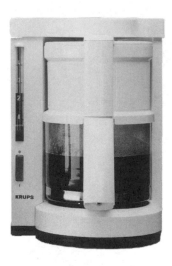

Café Prima #105

- Compact 4-cup (20 ounce) capacity
- Krups Exclusive "Deep Brew" Technology
- Compact design - great for small spaces
- Magnified water level indicator
- Non-stick warming plate
- Illuminated "On/Off" switch

Coffee Aroma Plus #134

- 12-Cup (60 ounce) capacity
- Two electronically-controlled brewing cycles for 1-3 or 4-12 cups
- Krups Exclusive "Deep Brew" Technology
- Aroma Savor lid seals the carafe to preserve flavor and heat
- Stop 'N' Serve feature
- Swing-Away double wall filter holder

ProCafé Time #212

- 10-cup (50 ounce) capacity
- 24-Hour Programmable Clock/Timer for "wake-up" coffee
- Programmable Auto Shut-Off in 1 to 5 hour increments
- Krups Exclusive "Deep Brew" Technology
- Stop 'N Serve feature
- Swing-Away double wall filter holder
- Non-stick warming plate
- Hidden cord storage

ProAroma Time #314

- 10-cup (50 ounce) capacity
- 24-Hour Programmable Clock/ Timer for "wake-up" coffee
- Aroma control cycle adjusts wattage for a rich 1-3 cup brew, medium 4-10 cup or strong 4-10 cup brew
- Programmable Auto Shut-Off in 1 to 5 hour increments
- Adjustable temperature control in 6 increments
- Carafe pre-warming feature
- LED readout for decalcification
- Krups Exclusive "Deep Brew" Technology
- Stop 'N Serve feature

CompacTherm #206
CompacTherm Deluxe #209

- 10-cup (50 ounce) capacity
- Double insulated thermal glass carafe keeps coffee hot up to 5 hours
- All-around stainless steel pour spout pours from any angle
- 24-Hour Programmable Clock/Timer (#209) for "wake-up" coffee
- Two electronically-controlled brewing cycles for 1-3 or 4-10 cups (#209)
- Auto Shut-Off at the end of the brewing cycle
- Krups Exclusive "Deep Brew" Technology
- Magnified water level indicator

Crystal Arome #398
Crystal Arome Time #458

- 10-cup (50 ounce) capacity
- Unique charcoal water filtration system removes unwanted chlorine taste
- 24-Hour Programmable Clock/Timer (#458) for "wake-up" coffee
- Programmable Auto Shut-Off in 1 to 5 hour increments (#458)
- Electronically-controlled brewing cycle for 1-3 or 4-10 cups (#398)
- Filtration indicator indicates when the filter should be changed
- Hermetically sealed carafe keeps coffee hotter and locks in coffee flavor

Duothek #264

- 2 x 10-cup (100 ounce) capacity
- Two independent brewing systems, great for entertaining
- One side with dual brewing cycles for 1-3 or 4-10 cups
- Krups Exclusive "Deep Brew" Technology
- Stop 'N Serve feature
- Front view water level indicator

Fast Touch Grinder #203

- 3 ounce capacity (up to 15 cups)
- Lid-activated safety feature
- Oval bean hopper for uniform grind
- Stainless steel cutting blades
- Easy pour lid

CompacTherm 10-Cup Stainless Steel Carafe #325

Unbreakable insulated stainless steel thermal carafe keeps coffee and other beverages hot up to 5 hours. Vacuum seal locks in flavor and aroma. Drip-free spout lets you pour from any angle.

Permanent Goldtone Filters

4-8 Cup #052 10-12 Cup #053 Micro screen "gold tone" mesh helps improve coffee taste. Saves paper, dishwasher safe.

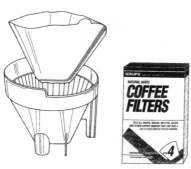

Paper Filters 100 Count

#983 Size 4 (10-12 cup)
#981 Size 2 (4-8 cup)
Made of the finest quality paper to filter out bitter coffee oils and sediment.

Coffee Dash #598

Four concentrated flavorings in one convenient jar for individual servings or full pots of flavored coffee. Hazelnut, Amaretto, Irish Cream and Chocolate Mint.

CHAPTER FOUR

HISTORY AND EVOLUTION OF THE ESPRESSO MACHINE

What Is Espresso?

Espresso is a method of quickly extracting the heart of the coffee flavor under pressure in single servings. Some believe the origin of the word is from the French "exprès" (especially for you), which may explain the common misspelling of espresso with an "x". Others cite the Italian "espresso" for rapid or fast as the source.

True espresso is a complex beverage, combining a special blend of coffee beans, darkly roasted, finely ground, densely packed and quickly brewed under pressure in individual servings. Properly brewed espresso with crema has a uniquely smooth and creamy, bittersweet flavor that captures the full essence of the beans.

What Is Crema?

Crema (schiuma in Italian) is the heart and soul of true espresso flavor. Crema is the foamy golden brown extraction that develops in the filter holder and encrusts the top of the espresso serving.

Delicate oils in the espresso grind form colloids, very fine suspended gelatin-like particles with a very slow rate of sedimentation. Overextracted espresso releases bitter oils that break down the colloids and dissipate the crema.

Crema is evidence that the right amount of fresh coffee was ground to the proper consistency, and a precise amount of water at the correct temperature was quickly forced under pressure through the fine espresso grind. A true espresso with crema is not easy to achieve, but the reward is well worth the effort.

The Evolution of Espresso

During the mid-1800's, a variety of large steam-operated commercial machines were developed in France and Italy. Tall and ornate boilers generated steam pressure to force water through a mechanical filter, producing large quantities of strong, pungent coffee.

In the early 1900's, Luigi Bezzera patented a steam pressure system that incorporated a filter holder and delivery group that brewed a single serving of espresso at one time. Desiderio Pavoni acquired Mr. Bezzera's patent and, in 1910, Pavoni began manufacturing these machines for commercial use in espresso bars and restaurants.

For more than 40 years the European café scene struggled along with this relatively low steam pressure until after WWII when Achilles Gaggia patented and introduced the first piston lever machine. To espresso lovers, this development was equivalent to the moment Alexander Graham Bell asked "Are you there, Mr. Watson?"

The piston lever machine was the first to produce espresso as we know it today. Pressure was developed by a spring-loaded lever and piston instead of steam pressure, eliminating the need to heat water above boiling to brew espresso. Two significant factors were the thermostatic control over the water brewing temperature and the ability to develop sufficient pressure with the piston lever to quickly force the water through a fine espresso grind.

Twelve years later, in 1961, Ernesto Valente developed the first commercial espresso machine which replaced the piston lever with an electric centrifugal pump to provide the pressure. The centrifugal pump supplied constant pressure of 9 bar to force the water through the espresso grind. Valente also used a heat exchanger to simultaneously control the separate brewing and steaming temperatures.

The use of a pump eventually made it possible to develop commercial machines that would operate automatically at the touch of a button. This technology also spurred the development of pump-driven home espresso machines that closely duplicated the results achieved by the larger commercial equipment found in cafés and restaurants.

Several Italian espresso machine manufacturers began producing pump-driven espresso machines for home use in the 1960's. Because of size and cost limitations, home-use pump-driven espresso machines do not use the constant pressure centrifugal pump or heat exchanger used in commercial equipment. Instead, pump-drive espresso machines for the home rely on what is referred to as a reciprocal pump, which operates somewhat like a pulsing solenoid.

The reciprocal pump in home machines produces pulsing pressure from 9 to 17 bar (135 to 250 psi). One bar (barometric pressure) equals roughly 14.69 pounds per square inch (psi) of pump pressure.

Other than the obvious difference in cost and size, one major difference between commercial and home-use machines is the "dwell time" or recovery period between brewing and steaming temperatures. Pump-driven espresso machines for the home require a recovery period to adjust between the separate temperatures for brewing and generating steam. Commercial equipment uses a heat exchanger or double boiler to avoid the dwell time, which increases the cost of commercial machines considerably.

One factor in increasing the interest in espresso in North America was the popularity of Italian restaurants in ethnic enclaves in cities like New York, Boston, Chicago, San Francisco and Toronto, where espresso is considered an absolute necessity by Italian patrons as an after-lunch or after-dinner beverage.

Another contributing factor during the 1960's and 1970's was the number of North Americans who visited Europe, specifically Italy, where they were introduced to the wonderful taste sensations of espresso, cappuccino, and caffè latte.

In most of Europe, cappuccino and caffè latte are considered breakfast drinks, rarely consumed past noon. But Americans embrace their milk-based espresso concoctions around-the-clock, probably because most are not really accustomed to the deep and penetrating bittersweet flavor of true espresso.

In the past 15 years there has been a virtual explosion of espresso bars and coffeehouses nationwide that seems to have spread from the Pacific Northwest. Today there are espresso machines located in fast food restaurants and convenience stores, department stores, books stores, beauty salons, apparel stores, and, in the Northwest, even dentist's offices and service stations serve espresso.

Espresso I.Q. Survey

Krups North America, Inc., commissioned an "Espresso I.Q." survey in 1993 through comprehensive telephone interviews with a total of 1,000 men and women across the country. Conducted by an independent market research firm, the Krups survey revealed that a vast majority of Americans (82%) correctly identified espresso as a "coffee drink that originated in Italy." Despite the misspelling of "espresso" in countless menus, the survey's majority realized that "espresso" is not spelled with an "x". Most Americans, however, mistakenly believed that one serving of espresso has more caffeine than a cup of regular coffee.

The small minority who "failed" the survey were rather imaginative in their ignorance about espresso. Five percent identified espresso as an "overnight delivery service," and four percent claimed that espresso is "the name of the public transportation system in Rome."

Cappuccino was correctly identified by a less distinguished majority of Americans (46%), with 2% mistaking this tasty beverage for a "pasta dish," and 9% confused caffè latte with biscotti (the traditional Italian twice-baked cookie served with espresso).

Another enterprising 9% believed that caffè latte is "a new chain of espresso cafés in the U.S.," while a third 9% of respondents considered the latte to be "a type of espresso machine."

The best grades went to people on the West Coast (56%) and our "Generation X" (18 to 34 year olds) with 53% for the highest Espresso I.Q.'s.

In 1993, the great majority of the survey's respondents nationwide (76%) still preferred a "regular coffee." Flavored coffee was chosen by 7% of all coffee drinkers, rising to 10% among women. Eight percent of respondents switched to cappuccino, with caffè latte the #1 preference among 12% of those residing on the West Coast.

As the popularity of espresso-related beverages continues to grow, the availability of espresso machines for the home increases. Now everyone can enjoy crema espresso, frothy cappuccino and smooth caffè latte in the comfort of their own home.

CHAPTER FIVE

HOME ESPRESSO EQUIPMENT

Home Espresso Equipment

A wide variety of home espresso and cappuccino equipment is available on the American market. Regardless of their price, style or brand name, electric home espresso machines fall into two basic categories: non-pump steam pressure and pump-driven systems.

An electric non-pump espresso machine relies on steam pressure generated in an encapsulated boiling chamber for brewing espresso and frothing milk. Pump-driven machines use an electromagnetic reciprocal pump to develop pressure between 9 and 17 bar (135 and 250 psi). The pump draws water from the water reservoir into either a boiler or Thermo-Block, and water is forced through the espresso grind under pump pressure. Thermostats maintain separate brewing and steaming temperatures in a pump-driven espresso machine.

Due to the increasing popularity of espresso and related beverages, manufacturers are continually developing new technology and more sophisticated systems for the home market.

The price of espresso equipment varies considerably, and some machines are more than double the price of others. Understanding how each different system operates will help you match machine features to your personal needs.

Non-Pump Espresso Machines

This is a pressurized non-pump boiler system, where water is heated in a sealed boiling chamber. The water is released either through the brew head for espresso, or through the steam arm for frothing. Some non-pump steam pressure machines have a simple On/Off Brewing Switch with a Steam Release Knob, while other machines feature a three-way control switch for Power On, Coffee, or Steam.

Because of their lower price, the electric non-pump steam pressure system is considered by many as a good entry level machine. There are certain limitations in terms of brewing true café-quality espresso with crema. However, this type of machine provides ample steam generation for a very respectable cappuccino, caffè latte, mocha or flavored steamer.

Pump Thermo-Block

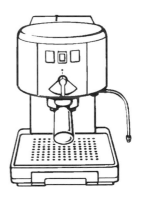

A relatively new innovation, the Thermo-Block is a radiator-like device that replaces the boiler. A 47" coiled channel in the Thermo-Block contains the heating element that flash-heats the water to separate, thermostatically-controlled brewing and steaming temperatures. A Thermo-Block system will brew café-quality espresso with crema, and provides continuous steam for cappuccino and lattes.

The pump operates in the steam mode on a Thermo-Block system and you can hear the pump pulsing water from the reservoir through the Thermo-Block. A user-friendly system, the Thermo-Block has a shorter wait or dwell time when switching from brewing to steaming temperatures.

Pump-Boiler System

The pump-boiler system for home use operates with a pump and heating element contained in a sealed boiler. The pump draws water from a reservoir into the boiler, and thermostats control the separate brewing and steaming temperatures. A pump-boiler system will brew café-quality espresso with crema, and provides generous steam for frothing milk.

The pump does not operate in the steaming mode on a pump-boiler system. Encapsulated steam is released from the top of the boiler through the steam arm only when the steam valve or dial is open. The wait time (also called dwell time) between brewing and steaming temperatures is slightly longer with a pump-boiler than a Thermo-Block system.

Combination Machines

The combination system incorporates an automatic filter drip coffee maker with the espresso/cappuccino features in one combined unit. This is a space saving appliance, very convenient for home entertaining. A certain number of guests will always prefer American drip coffee, while others may have developed a taste for espresso-related beverages.

The filter drip coffee and espresso systems operate independently or simultaneously. You may either brew just drip coffee or just espresso, or prepare both at the same time. (Note: you cannot brew espresso and froth milk at the same time on any home espresso machine.) Most combination machines feature the non-pump steam pressure espresso system with an automatic filter drip coffee maker.

Non-Pump Espresso Machines

Electric non-pump espresso machines represent the largest selling category of espresso machines in the number of units sold in North America. They are lower in price compared to pump-driven boiler or Thermo-Block machines, and, for that reason, this type of machine is considered by many to be an entry-level machine.

Most electric non-pump espresso machines have good steaming capabilities and will produce a very respectable cappuccino or caffè latte. But they do have certain limitations in connection with producing café-quality espresso with crema.

The non-pump machine relies on the steam pressure developed in a sealed boiler by heating water above 200°F. This develops pressure of approximately 3 bar (44 psi), considerably less than pump pressure. In addition, the high temperature used to create the steam pressure tends to scald the espresso and sometimes prohibits the development of crema.

You may wish to experiment with the consistency of the ground coffee to improve the flavor extraction, but do not use a grind too fine. With limited steam pressure, a fine grind may completely block the flow of water through the filter holder.

Most non-pump steam pressure machines will brew four espresso servings or two frothy cappuccino at one time from the 12 ounce boiling chamber.

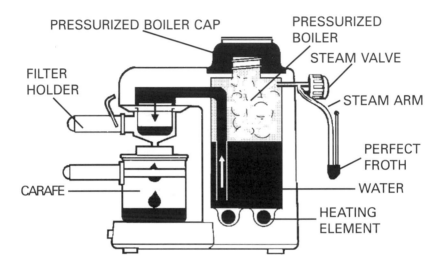

Once all of the water in the boiler has dissipated by brewing espresso and generating steam, it is necessary to turn off the machine and allow the unit to cool completely before removing the pressure cap to refill the boiler for additional servings of espresso or generating more steam. During the cool-down period, always depressurize the boiler by opening the steam valve or steam switch to relieve all of the remaining pressure.

IMPORTANT

Please keep in mind that an electric non-pump espresso machine is a pressurized boiler system. Under no circumstances should you attempt to loosen or remove the pressure cap or the filter holder until you have released all of the pressure in the boiler through the steam arm and allowed the machine to cool down completely.

STEP-BY-STEP GUIDE TO OPERATING A NON-PUMP STEAM PRESSURE MACHINE

> **IMPORTANT**
> The following guide is general in nature and not intended to supersede the instructions provided by the manufacturer of your machine. Please read your owner's manual carefully. Each machine has its own operating specifications and safety features. The name and location of switches and controls vary on each machine. Please refer to your factory instruction manual for the position and specific function of the controls related to your machine.

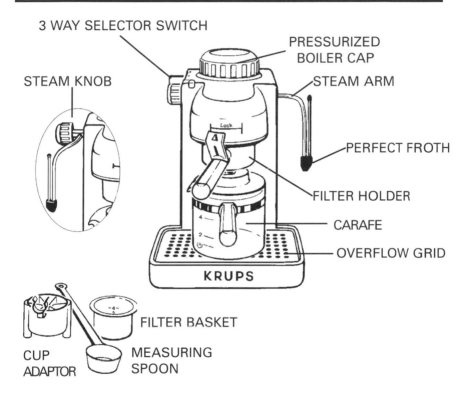

There are two basic types of non-pump steam pressure machines, and the difference relates to the placement and function of the controls and switches. The simplest version of this type of machine has an On/Off switch and a steam release knob. The second type of non-pump steam pressure machine has a three position switch to control brewing and steaming; Off, On/Coffee, and On/Steam. A three-way switch offers better control over the brewing and steaming functions.

Note: Before connecting the power cord to an electrical outlet, be sure that the Power Switch or the Selector Switch is in the "Off" or "O" position. This is important because when the machine is turned On, or in the Coffee position, the heating element is activated, and the heating element should not heat without water in the boiling chamber.

Preparing Espresso

Insert the coffee filter basket into the filter holder. You will note the markings "2" and "4" inside the filter basket which are coffee fill levels for either two or four cups of espresso.

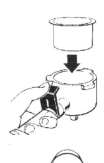

With the coffee measuring spoon, carefully fill the stainless steel coffee filter basket with ground espresso coffee to either the two-cup or four-cup level marked inside the coffee filter basket.

Use a relatively coarse grind for a non-pump steam pressure machine. If the grind is too fine or the coffee tamped too hard, the steam pressure cannot force the water through the bed of ground coffee.

Using the back of the measuring spoon, lightly tamp the coffee to level the surface of the grind in the coffee filter basket. Do not overfill the coffee filter basket which might cause clogging or overflow during the brewing process.

Wipe the edge of the filter holder with the palm of your hand or finger to remove any grounds that may affect the seal between the filter holder and the brew head.

Insert the filter holder into the brew head and turn to the right until it is firmly locked in place, in accordance with the instruction manual provided with your machine. If the filter holder is not seated and locked properly in the brew head it could become dislodged during the brewing cycle.

Remove the boiler cap and, using the glass carafe, fill the boiling chamber with fresh, cold water. Adjust the amount of water to the amount of coffee measured in the filter holder. Add extra water when you intend to also froth milk for cappuccino, but do not fill past the top metal band on the glass carafe.

Replace the boiler cap securely, turning clockwise for a tight seal. Place the lid on the carafe, and position the opening of the lid beneath the filter holder spout.

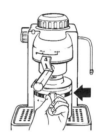

Note: Some machines are equipped with a two-cup adaptor that attaches to the filter holder to dispense espresso directly into two cups instead of the carafe.

You are now ready to brew espresso. Activate the brewing mode by turning the Power Switch to "On" or to the "Coffee" position if your machine has a three-way switch (the indicator light will illuminate). The heating element in the boiling chamber will begin to heat the water.

After approximately two minutes the water in the boiling chamber will have reached the proper brewing temperature, and the espresso will begin flowing into the carafe. Turn the Switch to the "Off" position when the espresso has finished brewing.

Preparing Cappuccino

If you intend to froth milk for cappuccino, or steam milk for caffè latte, it is recommended that you only brew espresso up to the steam mark on the glass carafe before steaming.

Brewing a measured amount of espresso before frothing creates more room at the top of the boiling chamber to generate steam. This also insures that you will not run out of steam during the frothing process.

When the espresso reaches the steam mark on the carafe, insert the steam arm just below the surface of cold, fresh milk in a frothing pitcher. Turn the switch to the steam position (or open the steam release valve).

The steam collected at the top of the boiler will be released through the steam arm into the pitcher of milk. Some machines feature an aerator or the "Perfect Froth" attachment, where air is induced into the steam to froth the milk without having to move the pitcher. For best results, do not allow the steam arm or frothing attachment to touch the bottom of the frothing pitcher.

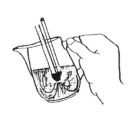

Without a "Perfect Froth" attachment, moving the pitcher in a circular motion or keeping the steam arm just below the surface of the milk may help aerate the froth.

After you have frothed or steamed the milk, return to the coffee brewing mode (or close the steam release knob) and the balance of your espresso will be dispensed into the carafe or, with the adaptor, into the espresso cups.

If you do not wish to brew espresso, and only froth milk for flavored steamers, turn to the steaming mode (or open the steam release knob) as soon as the machine is turned "On".

Some machines include a steam "build-up plug" to be inserted in the filter holder to direct the steam pressure through the steam arm.

Insert the steam arm just below the surface of the milk before steam begins to generate, to avoid splattering hot milk.

When you have finished brewing espresso and frothing milk, always turn the Power Switch to the "Off" position. Wipe the steam arm with a wet cloth to remove the milk coating.

Important: Do not remove the filter holder from the brew head or open the boiler cap until the machine has cooled down completely, in accordance with the instructions in your Owner's Manual.

During the cool-down period, always depressurize the boiling chamber by opening the steam valve or turning the three-way switch to the steam position to relieve all of the remaining pressure.

Pump-Driven Espresso Machines

Overview

If you are in pursuit of the ultimate espresso experience, you will need a pump-driven espresso machine. The elusive crema can only be produced under certain controlled conditions. A properly brewed espresso with crema is the base for any number of espresso-related beverages.

The many different elements required to properly extract a true crema espresso include the quality and freshness of the coffee, fineness of the grind, power of the espresso machine, controlled temperatures, tamping, timing, and even the quality of the water.

The entire process begins with an electric pump-driven espresso machine. However, even purchasing an expensive piece of equipment does not assure you will achieve café-quality espresso and cappuccino, unless you fine-tune your espresso making skills. Patience, trial and error will reward you with a skill that few Americans possess, and the lifelong pleasure of enjoying real espresso with crema at home.

Pump-Pressure

The pump used in home espresso equipment is a reciprocal (pulsing) pump that delivers varying pressure measured in barometric pressure (bar) and pounds per square inch (psi).

One (1) bar equals roughly 14.69 psi of pump pressure. As an object of comparison, the average water pressure supplied by city water departments to a kitchen faucet equals 35 psi. Depending on the size of the pump, pressure ranges from 9 to 17 bar or 135 to 250 psi.

Pressurized water follows the path of least resistance, and a fine grind forces the water to fully saturate the bed of ground coffee in the filter holder. The use of a fine espresso grind, leveled and tamped in the coffee filter basket of the filter holder inserted in the brew head, creates resistance and builds up pressure to force the water through the grind to extract only the heart of the espresso flavor.

While the heated water is in contact with the coffee, the oils in the espresso grind form colloids that result in the crema that should encrust the top of a properly brewed espresso serving.

If your espresso does not have crema, there could be several reasons. The coffee was not fresh, not ground to the proper consistency for your machine, not leveled and tamped in the filter holder, or the espresso was overextracted. Overextraction allows too much water to flow through the filter holder (more than 1-1/2 to 2 ounces per serving) which begins to extract some of the bitter oils that dissipate the crema.

Remember that you want to quickly extract only the heart and essence of the coffee flavor without overextracting. If you prefer your espresso lighter, dilute the serving with hot water from the steam arm to create an "espresso lungo."

Pump Thermo-Block System

The Thermo-Block resembles a radiator-like device with thin, coiled channels that flash-heat the water to the correct brewing or steaming temperatures. In the brewing mode, water is pumped from the water reservoir into the Thermo-Block where it is flash-heated to below boiling (from 192° to 197F°). The ready light indicates when the water has reached the correct brewing temperature. On some machines the ready light illuminates (usually green) and on other machines the ready light goes out (usually yellow or red) when the correct brewing temperature has been reached. A thermostat maintains this temperature until you are ready to brew espresso.

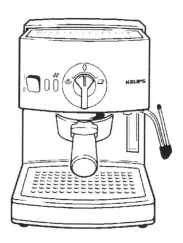

When the steam switch is activated, or the Selector Switch turned to the Vapore position, the heating element switches to a high heat setting to super-heat the Thermo-Block to the proper temperature for generating steam (250° to 275F°). The status or ready light may indicate when the high heat setting for steam has been reached. A second thermostat maintains this higher temperature until you are ready to froth or steam milk.

In a pump-driven Thermo-Block system, when the Selector Switch is turned to Vapore, or the Steam Valve is open, the pump draws water from the water reservoir and releases small droplets of water into the Thermo-Block in a fast sequence. These droplets of water are immediately transformed into steam by the high-heat thermostat in the Thermo-Block.

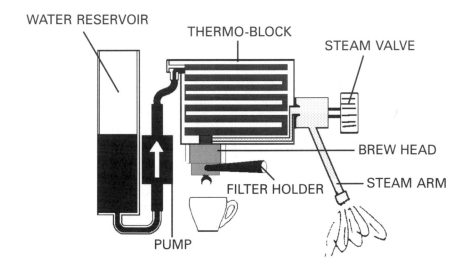

The pump continues to pulse as long as there is water in the reservoir in a Thermo-Block system when the machine is in the steam/Vapore mode. Steam is continuous with a Thermo-Block system, as long as there is water in the reservoir. You can tell if your machine is a pump Thermo-Block system by the pulsing of the pump during the steaming process.

After steaming, to return to the brewing mode, it is necessary to allow the thermostat to adjust the water temperature back to the brewing level (192° to 197°F) which is considerably below the high-heat steaming temperature. This is called the dwell time, which is generally shorter (30 seconds) with a Thermo-Block heating system.

STEP-BY-STEP GUIDE TO OPERATING A PUMP THERMO-BLOCK ESPRESSO MACHINE

> ### IMPORTANT
>
> The following guide is general in nature and not intended to supersede the instructions provided by the manufacturer of your machine. Please read your Owner's Manual carefully. Each machine has its own operating specifications and safety features. The name and location of switches and controls vary on each machine. Please refer to your factory instruction manual for the position and specific function of the controls and switches related to your machine.

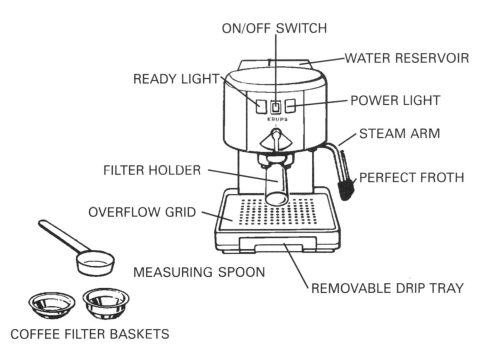

ON/OFF SWITCH

WATER RESERVOIR

READY LIGHT

POWER LIGHT

STEAM ARM

FILTER HOLDER

PERFECT FROTH

OVERFLOW GRID

MEASURING SPOON

REMOVABLE DRIP TRAY

COFFEE FILTER BASKETS

Important: Before connecting the power cord to an electrical outlet, be sure all controls are in the "Off" position. Fill the water reservoir with fresh, cold water.

Activate the Power Switch to the "On" position. The heating element will begin to heat the Thermo-Block to the correct temperature for brewing espresso.

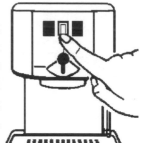

Wait until the ready light signals the thermostat in the Thermo-Block has reached the correct brewing temperature. On some machines the ready light will illuminate (usually green) and on other machines the ready light goes out (usually yellow or red) when the thermostat has reached the proper brewing temperature.

The thermostat maintains the temperature of the Thermo-Block from 192° to 197°F until you are ready to brew espresso.

Heat is an important factor in brewing a flavorful espresso. It is recommended that you allow your system to pre-heat for at least five minutes before brewing your first serving of espresso. Pre-heating the filter holder will further improve the flavor. Place the coffee filter basket (without coffee) in the filter holder and insert it into the brew head while the machine is pre-heating.

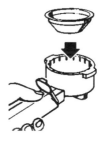

Always be sure that you have either the one- or two-cup coffee filter basket in the filter holder before inserting it in the brew head. Otherwise the filter holder may become dislodged as a result of the pressure generated in the brew head.

Fill the coffee filter basket with finely ground espresso coffee, one level measuring spoon or approximately 7 grams for one individual serving. Double this amount for the two-cup coffee filter basket. Do not overfill the coffee filter basket or the filter holder may not lock into the brew head.

Lightly tap the sides of the filter holder with the measuring spoon to evenly distribute the coffee in the coffee filter basket. Tamp the espresso grind by firmly depressing the back of the measuring spoon so that the bed of coffee is level and slightly compressed in the filter holder.

Pressurized water will follow the path of least resistance through the espresso grind, which is why tamping and leveling the coffee grind is important for full extraction of the espresso flavor.

Wipe the edge of the filter holder with the palm or your hand or finger to remove any grounds that may affect the seal between the filter holder and brew head.

Insert the filter holder into the brew head turning from left to right, in accordance with the manufacturer's instructions.

Place one or two pre-heated espresso cups under the filter holder spigots. If you are brewing a single serving of espresso, center the cup under the two spigots. For two servings of espresso, place two cups side by side, each directly beneath the spigots.

Turn the Coffee Switch to "On", or move the Selector Switch to the "Caffè" position. This activates the pump and you will begin hearing the pump pulsing action during the brewing process.

It should take about 15 to 20 seconds for the water to build up pressure in the brew head. You should then see a trickle of golden brown espresso flow into the cup(s).

As soon as you have extracted the desired amount of espresso, turn the Selector Switch to the "Off" position, or turn "Off" the Coffee Switch. This will stop the pulsing pump action and stop the flow of water through the filter holder.

To avoid overextraction you should only brew from 1-1/2 to 2-1/2 ounces of espresso for a single serving, and double that for a two-cup serving.

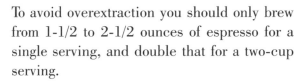

Remove the filter holder from the brew head and tap out the used espresso grounds in a grounds tray or waste bin.

Wipe the bottom of the brew head and shower disk with a damp cloth to remove any coffee residue. Priming through the brew head will also flush any residue that may have accumulated on top of the shower disk in the brew head.

If you proceed to frothing or steaming milk for cappuccino or caffè latte, please refer to Chapter 6 for complete frothing instructions.

Pump-Boiler System

The pump-boiler system replaces the Thermo-Block with a boiler that contains the heating element. The water is pumped from the water reservoir into the boiler where it is heated to below boiling (192° to 197°F) for brewing espresso.

A ready or status light will indicate when the water has reached the correct espresso brewing temperature, and a thermostat will maintain this temperature until you are ready to brew espresso. The ready light may cycle on and off during operation, which is normal and indicates that the heating element is cycling to maintain the correct brewing temperature.

It is important to induce water into the boiler of a pump-boiler system as quickly as possible after the Power is turned "On", since you do not want the heating element to heat in an empty boiler. When the Power Switch is in the "On" position, the heating element in the boiler is activated and will begin heating the water in the boiler to the brewing temperature.

Filling the boiler is normally referred to as priming the system, and merely requires that you activate the Coffee Switch, or turn the Selector Switch to the "Coffee" position, to energize the pump and begin pumping water from the reservoir into the boiler. You can tell the boiler is filled when water begins to flow through the brew head.

The sole function of the Coffee Switch or "Coffee" position on a pump-boiler system is to activate the pump to pump water from the reservoir into the boiler and through the brew head.

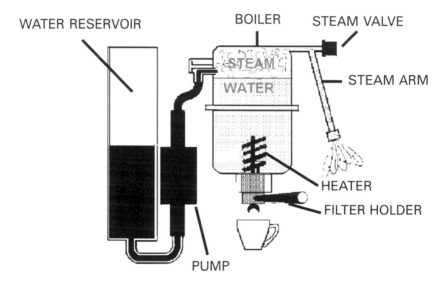

When the Steam Switch is activated, or the Selector Switch is turned to the "Steam" position, the heating element in the boiler switches to a high-heat setting and the water in the boiler is super-heated to a temperature ranging from 250° to 275°F.

Some machines feature a Steam Pre-heat Mode on the Selector Switch that activates the high-heat setting. A ready light will indicate when the correct temperature for steaming has been reached. A second thermostat maintains the high heat setting until you are ready to froth milk for cappuccino or steam milk for caffè latte. If the system has not reached the optimum steaming temperature, the first burst of steam may be weak and watery.

Steam accumulates in the top of the boiler and is not released through the steam arm until the Steam Valve is opened or the Selector Switch is in the "Steam" position.

You cannot generate steam unless there is water in the boiler, and the amount of steam generated at one time is related to the size of the boiler. If you are generating a great deal of steam without brewing espresso, the boiler may need refilling.

Do not confuse an empty boiler with the water level in the water reservoir. The boiler is located inside the machine and, even though there is water in the water reservoir, the boiler may need refilling.

This is accomplished in the same way as priming the system. Activate the Coffee switch or turning the Selector Switch to the "Coffee" position and the pump draws water from the reservoir into the boiler.

If you wish to brew espresso after steaming, it will be necessary to wait until the water in the boiler has cooled down from steaming to the brewing temperature from 192° to 197°F. This is referred to as the dwell time.

To shorten the dwell time, you may activate the Coffee Switch, or turn the Selector Switch to the "Coffee" position, which will then activate the pump drawing cool water from the reservoir into the boiler. This is the same as priming the system.

Drawing too much water from the reservoir into the boiler will cool down below the optimum brewing temperature, and you will then have a slight dwell time as the brewing thermostat adjusts the proper temperature to 192° to 197°F. A ready or status light will signal when the brewing temperature has been reached.

Step-by-Step Guide to Operating a Pump-Boiler Espresso Machine

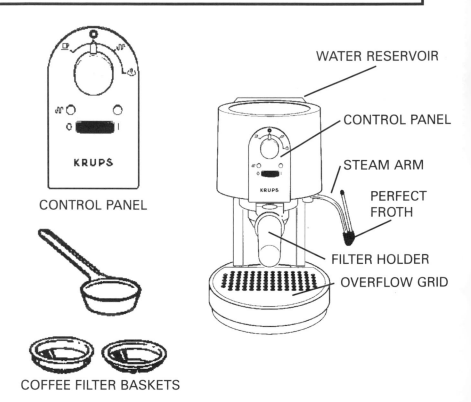

CONTROL PANEL

KRUPS

CONTROL PANEL

COFFEE FILTER BASKETS

WATER RESERVOIR

CONTROL PANEL

STEAM ARM

PERFECT FROTH

FILTER HOLDER

OVERFLOW GRID

Important: Do not activate the Power switch to the "On" position until you are ready to prime your system. Priming a pump-boiler machine primes the pump and induces fresh water into the boiler. The Power switch activates the heating element in the boiler and the heating element should not be activated until water has been drawn into the boiler from the water reservoir.

Priming A Pump-Boiler System

Make sure all controls are in the "Off" position before connecting the power cord to an electrical outlet. Fill the water reservoir with fresh, cold water. Place a cup under the brew head and simultaneously activate the Power On switch and turn the Selector Switch to the "Coffee" position (or activate the Coffee Switch). This will energize the pump to pump water from the water reservoir into the boiler.

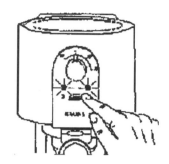

It is recommended that you allow several cups of water to flow through the system. In the case of a new machine, priming flushes out any dust that may have accumulated in the boiler in the manufacturing process. Priming the system also induces fresh water into the boiler and flushes out accumulated coffee residue from the brew head.

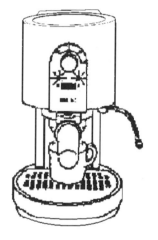

After priming the system, return the Selector Switch to the "Off" position (or turn off the Coffee switch). You are now ready to brew espresso.

Brewing Espresso Step-by-Step

The following steps assume that your machine is connected to an electrical outlet, that the water reservoir is filled with fresh, cold water, and the system has been primed in accordance with the manufacturer's instructions.

Activate the Power Switch to the "On" position. The heating element in the boiler will begin to heat the water in the boiler and the ready light will signal when the correct temperature for brewing espresso has been reached. On some machines the ready light illuminates (usually green) and on other machines the ready light goes out (usually yellow or red).

A thermostat maintains the temperature of the water in the boiler between 192° and 197°F until you are ready to brew espresso. The ready light may signal on and off, which is normal and indicates the thermostat is maintaining the correct brewing temperature in the boiler.

Heat is an important factor in brewing a flavorful espresso. It is recommended that you allow your system to pre-heat for at least five minutes before brewing your first serving of espresso. Pre-heating the empty filter holder by allowing it to rest in the brew head will further improve the flavor.

Always be sure that either the one- or two-cup coffee filter basket is in the filter holder before inserting the filter holder into the brew head. Otherwise the filter holder may become dislodged as a result of the pressure generated in the brew head.

Fill the coffee filter basket with finely ground espresso coffee. Use one level measuring spoon or approximately 7 grams of coffee for the one-cup coffee filter basket. Double this amount for the two-cup coffee filter basket. Do not overfill the coffee basket or the filter holder may not lock into the brew head.

Lightly tap the sides of the filter holder with the measuring spoon to evenly distribute the espresso. Tamp the espresso by firmly depressing the back of the measuring spoon to level and slightly compress the espresso in the coffee filter basket.

Pressurized water will follow the path of least resistance through the espresso grind, which is why leveling and tamping the grind is important for full extraction of the espresso with crema.

Wipe the edge of the filter holder with the palm of your hand or finger to remove any grounds that may affect the seal between the filter holder and brew head.

Insert the filter holder into the brew head and turn (usually from left to right) to lock the filter holder securely into the brew head. Refer to your Owner's Manual for detailed instructions regarding the insertion of the filter holder in the brew head.

Place one or two pre-heated espresso cups under the filter holder spigots. If you are brewing a single serving of espresso, center the cup under the two spigots. For two servings place two cups side by side, each directly beneath the filter holder spigots.

Activate the Coffee switch to the "On" position, or turn the Selector Switch to the "Coffee" position. This activates the pump and you will begin to hear the pump pulsing action during the brewing process.

It should take about 15 to 20 seconds for the water to build up pressure in the brew head. You should then see a trickle of golden brown espresso flow into the cup(s).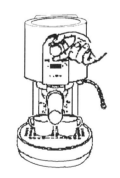

To avoid overextraction, you should only brew from 1-1/2 to 2-1/2 ounces of espresso for a single serving.

As soon as you have extracted the desired amount of espresso, turn "Off" the Coffee Switch, or return the Selector Switch to the "Off" position. This will stop the pump pulsing action and stop the flow of water through the filter holder in the brew head.

Remove the filter holder from the brew head and tap out the used coffee grounds in a grounds tray or waste bin. Use the thumb guard on the filter holder to keep the coffee filter basket inside the filter holder.

Wipe the underside of the brew head with a damp cloth to remove any coffee residue from the shower disk. Priming through the brew head will also flush any residue that may have accumulated on top of the shower disk.

If you proceed to frothing or steaming milk for cappuccino or caffè latte, please refer to Chapter 6 for complete frothing instructions.

What Went Wrong?

Espresso does not flow out of the filter holder:
    No water in the water reservoir
    Water reservoir not inserted properly
    Coffee ground too fine or tamped too hard
    Too much coffee in the coffee filter basket
    An air pocket is in the system

Espresso flows too quickly:
    Coffee ground too coarse
    Not enough coffee or not tamped
    Water had not reached the correct brewing temperature

Espresso spurts from around the filter holder:
    Filter holder not seated properly in the brew head
    Coffee grounds around the filter holder rim
    Too much coffee in the coffee filter basket
    Coffee ground too fine or tamped too hard
    Brew head gasket needs cleaning or replacing

Espresso has a bitter taste, no Crema:
    Coffee not fresh
    Grind needs adjustment
    System not pre-heated
    Coffee overextracted
    Shower disk needs cleaning

Espresso has scalded or burnt taste:
    Steam was produced first, and the temperature was
    not allowed to drop to the correct brewing temperature

Espresso not hot enough:
    Water did not reach the correct brewing temperature
    Filter holder, brew head and cups were not pre-heated

KRUPS

ESPRESSO MACHINE PRODUCT REVIEW

Espresso Mini #963

- Non-pump steam pressure system
- 4-cup (12 ounce) boiler capacity
- 4-cup carafe and 1 stainless steel filter basket
- Krups Patented "Perfect Froth" attachment for optimal frothing results, every time
- Steam build-up plug for steaming only
- 2-cup adaptor to brew directly into two cups
- Removable drip tray

An introductory machine for the espresso novice, prepare four espresso servings or two frothy cappuccino per cycle. Built-in safety valve in the boiling chamber pressure cap for safe operation.

Il Primo #972

- Non-pump steam pressure system
- Three-way switch easily controls brewing and steam
- 4-cup (12 ounce) boiler capacity
- 4-cup carafe and 1 stainless steel filter basket
- Krups Patented "Perfect Froth" attachment for optimal frothing results, every time
- 2-cup adaptor to brew directly into two cups
- Removable drip tray

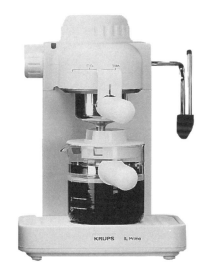

The three-way switch converts from brewing to steam instantly. Prepare up to four espresso servings or two cappuccino in the carafe or directly into cups, or just froth milk for hot chocolate and flavored steamers.

KRUPS ESPRESSO MACHINES

Novo Compact #989

- Pump-Boiler system
- 15 bar microchip monitored pump delivers perfect crema-laden espresso
- Stainless steel boiler
- Control dial with steam pre-heat mode
- Illuminated thermostat controls
- 34 ounce removable water reservoir
- Two stainless steel coffee filter baskets
- Krups Patented "Perfect Froth" attachment
- Removable drip tray and grid

This compact and easy-to-use espresso/cappuccino machine features a stainless steel boiler with pump pressure to prepare crema espresso, frothy cappuccino and smooth caffè latte. The four position control dial includes a steam pre-heat setting with ready lights for brewing and steaming temperatures.

Novo Compact Latte #882

- Pump-Boiler system
- 15 bar microchip monitored pump delivers perfect crema-laden espresso
- Stainless steel boiler
- Control dial with steam pre-heat mode
- Illuminated thermostat controls
- 34 ounce removable water reservoir
- Three stainless steel coffee filter baskets for 1, 2 or 4 cups of espresso
- 4-cup glass carafe holds 4-cups of crema espresso, or brew right into the carafe for easy one-step lattes
- Krups Patented "Perfect Froth" attachment
- Removable drip tray and grid

Steam milk directly in the glass carafe and brew two espresso servings for instant caffè latte - America's favorite. The user-friendly control dial includes a steam pre-heat setting. Brewing and steaming temperatures are controlled thermostatically.

Espresso Novo #964

- Pump-driven Thermo-Block system
- 15 bar microchip monitored pump delivers perfect crema-laden espresso
- 3-Way Selector Switch to instantly convert from brewing espresso to steaming milk
- 32 ounce removable water reservoir for continuous espresso making
- Two stainless steel coffee filter baskets
- Krups Patented "Perfect Froth" attachment
- Removable drip tray and grid

The sleek Euro-design of the Espresso Novo, along with its outstanding espresso making abilities, makes Espresso Novo America's #1 selling pump-driven espresso machine.

Espresso Pronto #988

- Pump-driven Thermo-Block system
- 15 bar microchip monitored pump delivers prefect crema-laden espresso
- 3-Way Selector Switch to instantly convert from brewing espresso to steaming milk
- Warming tray to pre-heat cups
- 37 ounce removable water reservoir for continuous espresso making
- Front view water level indicator
- Two stainless steel coffee filter baskets
- Krups Patented "Perfect Froth" attachment
- Removable drip tray and grid

The large 37 ounce water reservoir provides continuous "dry" steam through the Thermo-Block and no cold water discharge. Warming tray to pre-heat cups and visible front view water level indicator.

Espresso Maximo #863

- Pump-driven Thermo-Block system
- 15 bar microchip monitored pump delivers perfect crema-laden espresso
- Illuminated thermostat controls
- Control dial for espresso, steam or hot water
- Convenient built-in tamper
- Warming tray for pre-heating cups
- Large 60 ounce removable water reservoir
- Front view water level indicator
- Two stainless steel coffee filter baskets
- Krups Patented "Perfect Froth" attachment
- Removable drip tray and grid

Restaurant-quality results at home with the unique Thermo-Block system and microchip monitored steam pump. Great for entertaining, the control dial converts from espresso to steam and a hot water jet for tea or other hot beverages. Extra large 60 ounce water reservoir with built-in tamper.

Nespresso #986

- Pump-driven Thermo-Block system
- 19 bar pump with 11-15 bar extraction pressure range
- Brews using air-tight capsules of pre-measured coffee
- Control dial converts from brewing to steam instantly
- 42 ounce removable water reservoir
- Krups Patented "Perfect Froth" attachment
- Complete with two espresso cups and saucers
- Includes two sleeves of Nespresso coffee capsules

The state-of-the-art Nespresso system brews with patented capsules of pre-measured freshly ground coffee that are neat and easy to use. The powerful 19 bar pump delivers up to 11-15 bar of pressure in the brewing mode to extract the freshest flavor from the air-tight capsules.

Il Caffè Bistro #867

Combination Coffee and Espresso/
Cappuccino System

Ideal for the serious coffee lover, this combination machine offers endless possibilities from early morning eye-openers to after-dinner entertainment. Brew up to 10 cups of robust drip coffee and up to 4 espresso servings at the same time, or froth milk for cappuccino and lattes.

Coffee System Features:
- 10-cup (50 ounce) capacity
- 24-Hour Programmable Clock/Timer
- Auto Shut-off after 2 hours
- Stop 'N Serve feature
- Krups Exclusive "Deep Brew" Technology
- Swing-Away double wall filter holder

Espresso System Features:
- Non-pump steam pressure
- Three-way control switch for brewing and steam
- 4-cup glass carafe and 1 stainless steel filter basket
- Krups Patented "Perfect Froth" attachment

Perfect Froth #030

Unique, patented frothing attachment that aerates the milk by inducing more air to froth perfectly every time.

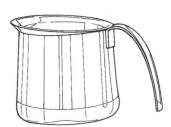

Frothing Pitchers

12 oz. Stainless Steel Frothing Pitcher #084

20 oz. Stainless Steel Frothing Pitcher #085

Heavy-gauge 18/10 stainless steel pitcher in 12 and 20 ounce capacities for frothing and steaming milk to perfection.

Flavored Syrups

Irish Cream Syrup #498 (12 oz. 375 ml)
Vanilla Syrup #497 (12 oz. 375 ml)
Almond Syrup #496 (12 oz. 375 ml)
Hazelnut Syrup #492 (12 oz. 375 ml)
4-Pack Assortment Mini Syrups #499

Cappuccino Topper #063

Four separate toppings for cappuccino and lattes in one convenient jar. Choose from Cinnamon, Vanilla, Chocolate and Pure Brown Cane Sugar.

Ceramic Cup & Saucer Sets

Classic Italian shape in ceramic to retain heat.
Available in Black, White, Teal Green and
Cobalt Blue

Espresso Cup & Saucer Set #050

Set of two 2-1/2 ounce espresso cups with matching saucers.

Cappuccino Cup & Saucer Set #051

Set of two 5 ounce cappuccino cups with matching saucers.

Double Latte Cup & Saucer Set #048

Set of two 16 ounce double latte cups with matching saucers.

CHAPTER SIX

Frothing
and
Steaming
Milk

Frothing & Steaming Milk

Overview

This chapter of the book should be of particular interest to North Americans because milk-based espresso beverages here are far more popular than straight espresso. The estimated percentage of straight espresso served in North America is only 10% to 15% of all espresso-related beverages, and this varies by region. The remaining 85% to 90% is an endless variety of milk-based drinks such as, cappuccino, caffè latte, flavored lattes, steamers, mochas, breves and iced espresso drinks.

Caffè lattes are currently outselling cappuccino in North America. By contrast, straight espresso is the traditional after-lunch and after-dinner drink in Italy and other Southern European countries. The reason for the overwhelming popularity of milk-based espresso drinks in North America may be due to improperly brewed espresso with a somewhat bitter flavor, which is commonly served here. The addition of hot milk or flavored additives covers the espresso deficiency.

In Europe milk-based espresso drinks are rarely consumed past noon. Europeans usually serve steamed (not frothed) milk with their espresso as a breakfast drink, called caffè latte in Italian, café au lait in French, café con leche in Spanish, and kaffe mit milch in German.

Milk-based espresso drinks fall into two categories; those that use a combination of steamed and frothed milk for cappuccino-type drinks, and steamed milk only for beverages like caffè latte and flavored steamers without espresso.

Steam is the clear vapor between hot water and a visible mist. Milk heated with live steam has a much better taste than milk heated in a saucepan over a burner on the stove. Heating milk with live steam alters the proteins of the milk and changes the texture for an improved taste.

In order to understand the difference between frothed and steamed milk, when you follow the instructions for frothing milk for cappuccino, you will note that the bottom half of the pitcher has steamed milk (without bubbles or froth) and the top half is frothed milk that has been highly aerated with small bubbles that form a foam or froth. Frothed milk has a thicker consistency than steamed milk.

Cappuccino derives its name from the order of Cappuchin monks recognized in Italy by their brown hooded robes, who originally developed this delicious combination of espresso with steamed and frothed milk. Frothed milk from the top of the steaming pitcher is spooned on top to "cap" the cappuccino and retain heat.

There are many variables in the art of frothing milk and each machine seems to have its own characteristics. With the advent of aerator-type devices, such as the "Perfect Froth" attachment, the whole concept of frothing milk has been greatly simplified. By immersing the tip of the "Perfect Froth" (which is attached to the steam arm) just below the surface of the milk (1/2"), the frothing process begins without any complicated manipulation of the frothing pitcher. The "Perfect Froth" aerates the milk by injecting additional air into the flow of steam.

Step-by-Step Guide to
Frothing Milk for Cappuccino

Always start with cold, fresh milk. Non-fat or 2% milk is easier to froth and delivers the best results. Whole milk, although slightly more difficult to froth, produces a denser, creamier froth. Warm or old milk will not froth. A chilled stainless steel frothing pitcher greatly assists in the frothing process. A stainless steel pitcher will chill in the freezer in just a few minutes.

With the Power switch "On", the water reservoir full, and the machine primed, activate the Steam Switch to On or turn the Selector Switch to the Vapore position. The thermostat controlling the heating element switches to the high-heat setting (250° to 275°F) to super-heat the water in the boiler or Thermo-Block for generating steam.

It will take from 30 to 60 seconds to convert the temperature from brewing (below 197°F) to the high-heat setting for producing steam. This adjustment period is called the "dwell time" which is generally faster on a Thermo-Block machine than a pump-boiler system.

On most machines, a ready or status light will indicate when the water in the boiler or Thermo-Block has reached the proper temperature for generating steam. A thermostat maintains this high-heat level until the Steam Switch or the Vapore position is turned "Off".

Now you are ready to froth milk for cappuccino.

Fill a pitcher 1/3 full of fresh, cold milk; the colder the better.

If your machine features a "Perfect Froth" attachment, which greatly assists in the frothing process, place the tip of the "Perfect Froth" just beneath the surface of the milk and open the Steam Valve or turn the Selector Switch to Vapore position.

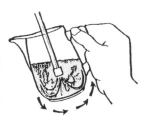

On a pump-boiler system, steam will immediately begin to flow from the steam arm into the frothing pitcher. With a Thermo-Block system you will hear a pump pulsing action and steam will begin to flow from the steam arm after 10 or 12 pump pulses.

If you do not have a "Perfect Froth" or aerator attached to the steam arm, moving the frothing pitcher in a circular or up-and-down motion will help aerate the milk and assist in the expansion of froth at the top of the pitcher.

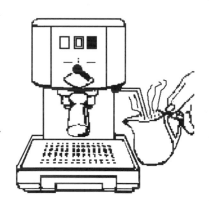

As the milk expands in volume, very slowly lower the pitcher keeping the steam arm just below the surface of the milk, to blend the froth thoroughly and eliminate large bubbles in the milk.

After the volume of milk in the pitcher doubles or triples, if necessary, you may further heat the milk by raising the pitcher and lowering the steam arm closer to the bottom of the pitcher.

This is a critical point in the frothing process. Be careful not to scald or boil the milk, which will dissipate the froth. The milk temperature for frothing should range between 135° and 150°F.

Turn off the Steam Valve (or return the Selector Switch to "0") before removing the pitcher from the steam arm, to avoid splattering hot milk. Tap the pitcher on the counter lightly and set it aside to settle the frothed milk on top of the steamed milk at the bottom of the pitcher.

Always open the Steam Valve or return to the Vapore position for a few seconds to allow a short burst of steam through the steam arm and evacuate any milk that may have been drawn up into the steam arm.

Wipe the steam arm with a wet cloth to remove any milk coating before it hardens. Hardened milk can be difficult to remove once it has solidified on the steam arm, and may cause the steam arm to clog.

If you are using a "Perfect Froth" attachment, remove the "Perfect Froth" from the steam arm and rinse in warm water. Be sure that the rubber tip of the straight arm of the "Perfect Froth" is not clogged, since this will close off the air flow and the "Perfect Froth" will not froth properly.

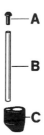

Ideally the frothed milk in the top half of the pitcher will be smooth and thick, and the froth should not dissipate quickly. A good froth consists of small bubbles and has a creamy texture. Underneath the froth is steamed milk.

The proportion of espresso to steamed and frothed milk for cappuccino is usually 1/3 espresso, 1/3 steamed milk, and 1/3 frothed milk on top to "cap" the cappuccino and retain the heat.

If you prefer a stronger coffee flavor, you may always alter the proportions to 1/2 espresso, 1/4 steamed milk and 1/4 frothed milk. Or, prepare a "dry" cappuccino with one shot of espresso and frothed milk, no steamed milk.

Using a spoon to hold back the froth makes it easy to pour steamed milk first, then spoon the frothed milk on top. Some prefer to pour the espresso from a separate cup over the steamed and frothed milk in a five-ounce cappuccino cup so that the espresso marks the white froth.

Steaming Milk For Caffè Latte & Steamers

The literal translation of the Italian caffè latte is coffee with milk. A classic caffè latte is 1/3 espresso with 2/3 steamed milk without froth.

Europeans usually prepare their morning coffee by pouring espresso and steamed milk together into a nine to 12-ounce breakfast cup, varying the proportions to personal taste. A traditional Swiss breakfast drink includes cubes of dried bread to make a type of porridge.

Caffè latte was first popularized in North America in the Pacific Northwest, mainly Seattle, and usually prepared with a slight variation to the European recipe. Most lattes served here have a dollop of frothed milk layered on top and, more recently, with flavored syrups added.

There is a fine line between a cappuccino and a caffè latte, usually related to the size of the serving and proportion of froth to steamed milk. Another version of an expanded cappuccino is the "latteccino" with more frothed milk added to the latte.

A caffè latte has more than half steamed milk and is usually served in a larger cup with a capacity from nine to 12 ounces. Cappuccino is usually served in a five-ounce cup or glass with equal thirds of espresso, steamed milk, and frothed milk.

In general, when steaming milk for lattes, start with more milk in the frothing pitcher than when frothing for cappuccino. Flavorings dissolve better when added to the cup before espresso, or blended with milk when steaming.

Not all drinks need espresso. Even a classic hot chocolate tastes better using milk heated with live steam. Steamers are made by steaming flavored milk without espresso. Flavored lattes and steamers are gaining in popularity.

CHAPTER SEVEN

RECIPES
CLASSIC
&
CONTEMPORARY

Classic & Contemporary Recipes

Coffee is an expression of hospitality throughout the world. Whatever the occasion, from early morning eye-openers to after-dinner entertaining, coffee is meant to be enjoyed at any time of day. Hot or cold, flavored or straight, coffee is a versatile complement that blends perfectly with an endless variety of ingredients.

Most iced coffee drinks are similar to the hot version and, therefore, most of the following recipes can also be served cold by adding ice in a tall glass. By blending these same drinks with ice in a blender they become a frothy cooler, similar to granitas.

Coffee Sugars

Flavored sugar is an elegant way to sweeten any coffee drink. Sprinkle one cup of sugar with one teaspoon grated lemon or orange rind and mix well. Or, bury two whole vanilla beans in one pound of granulated sugar. Cinnamon, nutmeg and cloves can also be used for flavoring sugar. Stored in an air-tight container in the refrigerator, flavored coffee sugar will keep for several weeks.

Drip Coffee Entertaining Ideas

Banana Shake

Cut 1 banana in chunks and combine with 1-1/2 cups cooled coffee and 3 tbs. sugar in the blender at high speed. When smooth, add 1 cup vanilla ice cream and blend at medium speed.

Irish Coffee

In a tall glass, mix eight parts coffee to one part whisky and add sugar to taste. Prepare thickened cream by whipping fresh cream until it thickens but can still be poured. Gently pour the thickened cream over an inverted spoon to float the cream on the surface of the coffee. Do not stir, but sip the warm Irish Coffee through the cold layer of whipped cream.

Café Brûlot

An hour before serving, pour 1 ounce Galliano, 1 ounce Curacao and 1-1/2 ounces brandy into a deep saucepan. Add 6 lemon peel and 6 orange peel, 6 whole allspice, 4 whole cloves and 2 cinnamon sticks broken in half. Heat this mixture over a low heat. Slowly warming releases the flavors in the spices but a heat too high will evaporate the alcohol. Turn off the heat. Just before serving, heat the liqueurs again. Brew six servings of rich, drip coffee. When the liqueurs are hot, light with a match to flame for one or two minutes. Pour the coffee into the saucepan and reheat, but do not boil. Spoon the Café Brûlot into coffee cups and add one piece of lemon and orange peel to each serving.

Classic Espresso Recipes

Espresso

A single serving of espresso, roughly 1-1/2 ounces, served in a 2-1/2 ounce, pre-heated demi-tasse cup.

Espresso Ristretto

A short or "restricted" espresso, where the flow of water through the brew head is stopped at roughly 1 ounce per serving.

Espresso Lungo

A single serving of espresso diluted with 4 ounces of hot water to produce a milder or "long" espresso. Also called an "Americano" the espresso is diluted with hot water from the steam pipe, not from the brew head, to resemble American drip coffee but with a richer espresso flavor.

Espresso Doppio

A double serving of espresso, from three to four ounces. Use the two-cup coffee basket in the filter holder and serve in a five-ounce cappuccino cup.

Espresso Macchiato

A single serving of espresso "marked" with a tablespoon of frothed milk.

Espresso Con Panna

A single or double espresso serving topped with whipped cream and garnished with chocolate.

Espresso Romano

A single serving of espresso served with a fresh lemon peel. Serve the lemon peel on the saucer, not in the espresso, since the citrus acid will dissipate any crema.

Espresso Coretto

A single serving of espresso that is "corrected" with a dash of liqueur or spirits.

Contemporary Espresso Recipes

Cocoa Mint Espresso Shake

In a blender, mix 1 espresso serving, 1 teaspoon crème de cacao, 1/2 teaspoon crème de menthe, and 1 scoop vanilla ice cream for 15 to 20 seconds until smooth.

Espresso Vanilla Delight

Combine four servings of espresso (roughly 8 ounces), 1 cup milk, 1 teaspoon vanilla, and 1/4 cup sugar. Stir until the sugar is dissolved and chill. When ready to serve, scoop vanilla ice cream in a glass and pour the espresso mixture over the ice cream. Top with whipped cream and garnish with shaved chocolate.

Almond Iced Espresso

Combine 1 serving of espresso, 1 cup of milk, 1 teaspoon vanilla syrup, 1 teaspoon almond syrup, and 1/2 teaspoon sugar. Pour into a tall glass filled with ice cubes, and garnish lightly with ground cinnamon.

Nightcap Espresso

Combine 2 sugar cubes, 2 whole cloves and 2 ounces Bourbon in a warm mug. Fill with a double (doppio) espresso and stir with a cinnamon stick. Consider decaf espresso for those adversely affected by caffeine.

Classic Cappuccino Recipes

Cappuccino reportedly takes its name from the chocolate hues of the robes worn by the Capuchin monks in Italy who favored this delicious dessert coffee. Cappuccino can be tailored to one's own taste by adjusting the proportion of steamed milk and froth. Topped with cinnamon, chocolate or even liqueur, its versatility makes cappuccino a worldwide gourmet choice.

Cappuccino

A classic cappuccino is 1/3 espresso, 1/3 steamed milk, and 1/3 frothed milk served in a five-ounce, pre-heated cappuccino cup. The froth on top of the steamed milk is spooned onto the serving to "cap" the drink and retain heat.

Mocha

By dissolving powdered cocoa or chocolate syrup in fresh, cold milk before frothing, a classic cappuccino becomes a mocha.

Cioccolaccino

Place a thick slice of orange in a cappuccino cup. Prepare a cappuccino, pouring the espresso over the sliced orange, adding steamed milk and topping with frothed milk. Garnish with grated orange peel or ground cinnamon.

Contemporary Cappuccino Recipes

Cappuccino des Artistes

Beat 1 cup heavy sweet cream until it holds soft peaks. Add 2 tablespoon sugar and 1 teaspoon vanilla and beat until stiff. Beat 2 egg whites until stiff and add to the cream mixture. Divide the cream blend into three cappuccino cups and add a fresh espresso serving to each cup.

Peanut Butter Mocha

Add 1 heaping tablespoon of smooth peanut butter to a thick chocolate syrup in a five-ounce cappuccino cup and blend well. Add espresso and stir. Froth milk in a steaming pitcher and, holding back the froth with a spoon, pour steamed milk into the espresso mixture. Spoon the froth onto the Peanut Butter Mocha and garnish with chocolate sprinkles.

Hazelnut Cappuccino

Pour 1/2 ounce hazelnut syrup into a five-ounce cappuccino cup. Add espresso, stir, and add steamed milk. Top with frothed milk and garnish with vanilla powder.

Vanilla Cappuccino

Pour 3/4 ounce vanilla syrup in a steaming pitcher and fill 1/3 full with fresh, cold milk. Froth the vanilla and milk mixture. Add the steamed milk to an espresso serving in a pre-heated five-ounce cappuccino cup. Top with frothed milk and sprinkle with cocoa.

Classic Caffè Latte Recipes

The literal translation of the Italian "caffè latte" is coffee with milk and, in Italy, coffee means espresso. Known by the French as Café au Lait, a classic caffè latte is 1/3 espresso to 2/3 steamed milk, or a doppio (double) espresso with five ounces of steamed milk served in a large nine-ounce cup or wide-mouthed glass.

Latteccino is a cross between a cappuccino and a latte, for an Americanized caffè latte with frothed milk spooned on top of the espresso and steamed milk.

Caffè Breve

Substituting Half-n-Half for milk turns a classic caffè latte into a breve. Half-n-Half or cream will not froth due to the higher fat content, but steaming cream for breves adds an even richer texture than steamed milk.

Latte Macchiato

Prepare a glass of steamed milk and slowly dribble a single serving of espresso over the top to "mark" the milk with espresso.

Steamer

Steamed milk that has been flavored with syrup, served without espresso, becomes a steamer or flavored latte sans espresso.

Contemporary Latte Recipes

French Vanilla Double Latte

Pour 1/2 ounce hazelnut syrup and one ounce vanilla syrup in a large 12-ounce breakfast cup or latte glass. Prepare a doppio (double) espresso serving and add to the syrup mixture. Steam milk with a slight foam on top and, holding back the froth with a spoon, fill the cup with steam milk. Spoon the layer of froth on top and garnish with cocoa or chocolate sprinkles.

Almond Breve

Pour one ounce of almond syrup in a latte cup. Brew a doppio (double) espresso serving into the cup. Steam Half-n-Half and fill the cup. Substituting steamed milk for Half-n-Half becomes an Almond Latte.

Cocoa Mint Caffè Latte

Add 1 teaspoon crème de menthe and 2 teaspoons crème de cacao to a latte cup. Prepare a classic caffè latte, adding the espresso to the syrups first and filling the cup with steamed milk. Top with a layer of frothed milk and garnish with chocolate. Mixing this beverage in a blender with two scoops of vanilla ice cream becomes a smooth, chilled Cocoa Mint Latte Shake.

Latte Lingo

The social culture surrounding espresso has created a language all its own. In Italy, if you order just a "latte" you will be served a glass of milk. Ordering just a "latte" in North America now includes a long list of variations we are calling "latte lingo".

Latte	Standard latte in an 8-ounce cup
Short	Small latte in a 5-ounce cup
Tall	Large latte in a 12-ounce cup
Grande	Extra large in a 16-ounce cup
Double Short	Double shot of espresso in a 5-ounce cup
Double Tall	Double shot of espresso in a 12-ounce cup
Tall Skinny	Large latte made with non-fat milk
Tall Two	Large latte made with 2% milk
Harmless	Latte using decaffeinated espresso
Skinny Sleeper	Latte with decaf and non-fat milk
Foamless	Latte with steamed milk, no froth
Steamer	Flavored latte without espresso
Breve	Latte with Half-n-Half instead of milk
Wet	Cappuccino with steamed and frothed milk
Dry	Cappuccino with frothed milk only
Americano	Espresso diluted with hot water

The list goes on, and everyone can join the fun; from steamers for kids, to skinnies for calorie counters. After experimenting with the preceding recipes, you may find yourself using the same lingo to describe your own signature drinks.

CHAPTER EIGHT

CARE
AND
MAINTENANCE

Care and Maintenance

Filter Drip Coffee Maker

Your filter drip coffee maker should be kept immaculately clean in order to function properly and consistently produce rich, flavorful coffee. Coffee, especially a dark roast, may impart a gummy residue that may collect in the filter holder, the carafe lid and the glass carafe. A build-up of this gummy residue may eventually taint the coffee flavor.

Most filter drip coffee systems have only three removable parts; the filter basket which holds either the paper or mesh coffee filter, the glass carafe and carafe lid. These components should be washed in a solution of hot water and mild liquid soap. Although these components are usually dishwasher safe on the upper rack, you should check your Owner's Manual to verify the manufacturer's recommendation for use of the dishwasher.

Do not use an abrasive or scouring agent on any coffee maker components or the body of the machine itself. Never immerse the appliance in water or any other liquid. To clean the housing, wipe the machine with a soft damp cloth.

To clean the water chamber, just rinse with cold water periodically. Do not use a cloth or paper towel to dry the inside of the water chamber, since this may leave fuzzy deposits in the chamber that could be drawn into the brewing system.

Decalcifying

The filter drip coffee maker will periodically need decalcifying to remove calcium (limestone) deposits that accumulate in the brewing system. These minerals are always present to some degree in drinking water. In areas where the water is very hard (a high content of minerals), decalcifying will be necessary more often than in areas with softer water.

You can tell when decalcification is necessary by an obvious slow-down in the coffee brewing cycle. The frequency of decalcification will depend on the type of water and how often the machine is used. More sophisticated filter drip coffee brewers now feature an status light that indicates when the machine needs decalcification.

Periodically decalcifying your filter drip coffee maker will prolong the life of your machine.

How To Decalcify

A liquid or powder decalcifying agent specifically designed for a filter drip coffee system is recommended. These decalcifying solutions can usually be purchased from the retailer where you bought your machine. In some cases decalcifiers are also available directly from the manufacturer of your filter drip coffee system. Always follow the instructions in your Owner's Manual supplied by the manufacturer for the decalcifying procedure for your machine.

As a general rule, dissolve the contents of the decalcifier in two cups of cold water. Pour this solution into the water chamber and place the empty carafe on the warming plate. Press the Coffee "On" Switch.

Allow the water to cycle completely from the water chamber through the empty filter holder basket into the glass carafe. Repeat this procedure two or three times to completely flush out any calcium or limestone deposits.

When you have finished decalcifying, always run four to eight cups of clear, cold water through the brewing cycle to remove any traces of the decalcifying solution.

Espresso Machines

It is especially important that an espresso machine be kept immaculately clean in order to function properly and consistently produce flavorful espresso with crema. Espresso coffee is usually a darker roast and imparts a gummy residue that may eventually taint the espresso flavor. This residue collects in the filter holder, coffee filter baskets, and especially on both the top and bottom surfaces of the perforated shower disk attached to the bottom of the brew head.

To reduce the frequency of shower disk cleaning, always flush hot water through the brew head and wipe the bottom of the shower disk with a damp cloth after each espresso session to remove any accumulation of coffee residue.

Wash all removable parts that come in contact with the espresso (filter holder, coffee filter baskets, drip tray and grid) in a solution of warm water and mild liquid soap. Be sure to rinse these components thoroughly since a soapy residue may taint your coffee flavor. Do not use harsh soaps, detergents or abrasives to clean any components. It is not recommended that any of these components be put in the dishwasher due to the harsh detergents and high heat generated in the drying cycle.

Remove and empty the water reservoir, rinse with fresh water and let it air dry. Do not dry the water reservoir with a cloth or paper towel which may leave fibers in the reservoir that could be drawn into the brewing system. Never immerse the body of the espresso machine in water or any other liquid. Wipe the machine housing with a soft damp cloth.

After frothing milk, wipe the steam arm with a damp cloth to remove any milk coating before it hardens. To prevent milk from hardening inside the steam arm, always evacuate a short burst of steam through the steam arm after frothing to purge any milk that may have been drawn into the steam arm.

If milk hardens inside the steam arm, the power of the steam will diminish. Immerse the steam arm in a pitcher of warm water and let it soak overnight, or "froth" hot water to soften any milk coating. In extreme cases, insert a needle or thin wire into the steam arm to loosen and remove any milk deposits.

Cleaning the "Perfect Froth" Attachment

The top closure of the straight arm of the "Perfect Froth" attachment has a very fine suction hole that draws air into the milk. The "Perfect Froth" will not perform properly when milk is drawn into this opening (A). If this small opening is clogged, insert a fine needle to remove any milk deposits.

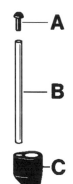

To clean the "Perfect Froth", remove the attachment and disassemble the three parts A, B, C. Rinse in warm water (without soap), reassemble and attach the "Perfect Froth" to the steam arm.

Periodic Brew Head Cleaning

One of the most important maintenance procedures for a pump-driven espresso system is the periodic cleaning of the perforated shower disk. The frequency depends on how often you use the machine.

You can tell when some of the perforations are clogged by observing the flow of water from the brew head through the shower disk without the filter holder in place. If water does not flow through the brew head evenly, the perforations of the shower disk may be clogged.

To remove the shower disk for cleaning, it is important to follow the instructions in your Owner's Manual. Most manufacturers recommend that you carefully remove the center screw or bolt with a screw driver or allen wrench. Do not force the screw, which can strip the threads. If the screw is difficult to turn, switch the Power "On" and allow the brew head to heat up. Be careful; the parts will be hot.

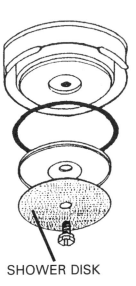

Clean the shower disk under hot running water, or immerse it in a saucepan of boiling water. Re-assemble per the instructions provided in your Owner's Manual.

SHOWER DISK

To retain a tight seal between the filter holder and brew head, do not store the filter holder in the brew head when the machine is not in use.

Decalcifying An Espresso Machine

Remember that an espresso serving is 98% water and the quality of the water affects the flavor of the espresso and the extraction of crema. If your water supply has a high mineral content (hard water) it is strongly recommended that you use filtered or bottled water to eliminate the build-up of calcium and mineral deposits. The use of bottled water will always improve the flavor of your espresso, especially in areas where the water supply is highly chlorinated.

One of the most common causes of espresso machine service problems is the accumulation of calcium and mineral deposits in the internal working components of the espresso machine. This problem is similar to decalcifying a steam iron or filter drip coffee system.

A build-up of calcium in the brewing system will diminish the power in the brewing and steam modes, and can eventually damage the machine. Calcium deposits collect inside the channels of a Thermo-Block system, or around the heating element inside the boiler of a pump-driven boiler system.

There are several espresso machine decalcifiers on the market specially designed for espresso brewing systems. Please refer to your Owner's Manual before decalcifying your machine, since there will undoubtedly be specific instructions provided by the manufacturer for decalcifying your particular system.

Once you have added the solution to your water reservoir, remove the filter holder and flush the solution through both the brew head and steam arm. It may be necessary to repeat this process several times to completely remove deposits that accumulate in the system. After decalcifying, rinse the water reservoir and refill with fresh, cold water. Use the same procedure through both the brew head and steam arm to remove all traces of the decalcifier.

After Sales Service

Every manufacturer of home espresso equipment provides specific instructions in their Owner's Manual to resolve common malfunctions of a machine. In some cases they will be able to troubleshoot over the phone, such as advising you to decalcify the machine.

Do not attempt to repair your machine at home. If you are not certain of the procedure for repair of your particular machine, call the manufacturer for more specific instructions.

If the problem cannot be resolved over the phone, the manufacturer may require that the machine be carefully packed and taken to a nearby factory authorized service center. The following tips will help expedite the repair and return of your machine:

Keep all removable parts at home to avoid further damage in transit or loss of parts. Pack the appliance carefully, in the original carton, if possible.

Tape a legible note to the body of the machine with your name, address, phone number, model number of your machine and a brief explanation of the problem.

To insure in-warranty service, you may need to provide the date or proof of purchase. Repair work for after warranty service is usually billed for materials and labor.

KRUPS SPARE PARTS LISTING

Should the need arise for repairs or replacement parts (within or after the warranty period), please call the KRUPS Customer Service Department.

Call toll free 1-800-526-5377

KRUPS Replacement Parts & Accessories

Style No. Description   Fits KRUPS Model Nos.:

Automatic Filter Drip Coffee Makers

Replacement Carafes:

Style No.	Description	Fits KRUPS Model Nos.:
016-42	10-Cup Carafe Black	182, 201, 212, 321
016-70	10-Cup Carafe White	182, 201, 212, 321
018-42	10-Cup Carafe Black	170
018-70	10-Cup Carafe White	170
025-42	10-Cup Carafe Black	150
025-70	10-Cup Carafe White	150
034-42	10-Cup Carafe Black	178, 264, 130, 136, 140, 145, 149, 312, 313, 314
034-70	10-Cup Carafe White	178, 264, 130, 136, 140, 145, 149, 312, 313, 314
035-42	12-Cup Carafe Black	134, 137, 141
035-70	12-Cup Carafe White	134, 137, 141
589-42	10-Cup Carafe Black	498, 398
077-42	4-Cup Carafe Black	105
077-70	4-Cup Carafe White	105

Insulated Carafes:

Style No.	Description	Fits KRUPS Model Nos.:
281-42	CompacTherm Black	270
281-70	CompacTherm White	270
282-42	CompacTherm Black	206, 209
282-70	CompacTherm White	206, 209
325-75	Stainless Steel	206, 209, 339

Coffee Flavorings:

Style No.	Description
492	Hazelnut Syrup 12.7 oz. (375 ml)
496	Almond Syrup 12.7 oz. (375 ml)
497	Vanilla Syrup 12.7 oz. (375 ml)
498	Irish Cream Syrup 12.7 oz. (375 ml)
490	4-Pack Assorted Mini Syrups
598-01	Coffee Dash Jar

KRUPS SPARE PARTS LISTING

Replacement Filters & Water Filtration Kits:

052	Goldtone Filter #2	170, 158, 171, 987
053	Goldtone Filter #4	10 and 12 Cup Models
981	Paper Filter #2 (100)	For 4, 6, and 8 Cup Models
983	Paper Filter #4 (100)	10 and 12 Cup Models
590	Charcoal Filters (2)	458, 398
593-42	NaturActiv Kit White (Housing + 1 Filter)	313, 314
593-70	NaturActiv Kit Black (Housing + 1 Filter	313,314
594-00	2 NaturActiv Filters	313, 314
595	Crystal Arome Kit (Charcoal Filter, 80 paper filters, decalcifier)	458, 398

Espresso/Cappuccino Replacement Carafes

022-42	Carafe Black	996
027-42	Espresso Carafe Blk	171, 865, 866, 867, 963, 972, 987, 993
027-79	Espresso Carafe Wht	171, 865, 866, 867, 963, 972, 987, 993
033-42	Coffee Carafe Black	171, 987
033-70	Coffee Carafe White	171, 987
036-42	Coffee Carafe Black	865, 866, 867
036-70	Coffee Carafe White	865, 866, 867

Espresso/Cappuccino Accessories

030	Perfect Froth Attachment
050	Espresso Cup & Saucer Set/2 (Black, White, Teal Green, Cobalt Blue)
051	Cappuccino Cup & Saucer Set/2 (Black, White,Teal Green, Cobalt Blue)
048	Double Latte Cup & Saucer Set/2 (Black, White,TealGreen,CobaltBlue)
063	Cappuccino Topper: Cinnamon, Vanilla, Chocolate & Sugar
084	12 oz. Stainless Steel Frothing Pitcher
085	20 oz. Stainless Steel Frothing Pitcher
492	Hazelnut Syrup 12.7 oz. (375 ml)
496	Almond Syrup 12.7 oz. (375 ml)
497	Vanilla Syrup 12.7 oz. (375 ml)
498	Irish Cream Syrup 12.7 oz. (375 ml)
499	4-Pack Assorted Mini Syrups

CHAPTER NINE

FILTER DRIP COFFEE AND ESPRESSO

A

aerator Device attached to the steam arm that aerates milk by inducing additional air into the flow of steam. More air in the jet of steam creates more bubbles in the milk to increase the volume rapidly and "froth" the milk. See "Perfect Froth".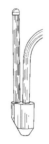

atmosphere (ATM) Unit of measuring pump pressure; one atm (atmosphere) equals 14.69 psi (pounds per square inch) of pump pressure. The preferred pump pressure for a home espresso machine is between 9 and 17 ATMS (x 14.69 - 132 to 250 psi). The European term for ATM is Bar for barometric pressure.

arabica (coffea arabica) A coffee bean that originated in Ethiopia, noted for its intense, aromatic flavor. Used in specialty coffees, arabica beans are lower in caffeine, more expensive, and have more flavor and aroma than "robusta" beans. Arabica beans are also called high-grown because the coffee trees are grown 3,000 feet above sea level.

Americano An espresso that resembles American drip coffee by adding hot water from the steam arm to dilute the serving but preserve the espresso flavor. This should not mean overextracting espresso by allowing more water to flow through the brew head. In Italy "Americano" refers to an espresso lungo or long pull.

B

bar   The unit of measure used in Europe for pump pressure as opposed to atmospheres (ATM) or psi. Barometric pressure is slightly less than atmospheric pressure, and one bar is very close to one ATM of pressure.

Barista   Italian word for one who has mastered the espresso machine, and an expert on brewing and mixing espresso beverages.

blend   Mixing two or more straight coffee (varietals) from different origins after the beans have been roasted. Different roasts (lighter and darker) are blended either by the roaster or specialty coffee retailer, and, with a quality roast, the blend is a matter of personal taste. "House Blend" refers to the special blend a roaster or retailer has developed by mixing different beans to their preference.

boiler   A closed vessel used to heat water or generate steam in espresso machines. Home espresso machines are available in a variety of boiler sizes, and the capacity is measured in milliliters. The capacity and materials used to construct the boiler impact on the cost and operation of the espresso machine. Boilers are constructed of aluminum, stainless steel, brass or copper.

brew head   The brewing chamber that holds the filter holder in place and dispenses water through the espresso grind. The brew head with the filter holder is called the delivery group. The brew head is attached to the bottom of the boiler or Thermo-Block with the shower disk and gaskets to create a tight seal around the filter holder to build up pressure when brewing espresso.

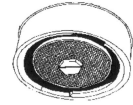

burr(s) Two corrugated steel cylindrical plates with cutting edges used in coffee grinders to slice or shave the coffee bean to a uniform grind. The top burr is stationary and the bottom burr rotates. An electric burr grinder uses a motor to control the speed of the burrs, reducing heat and dissipation of coffee oils in grinding. The burrs control the consistency of the grind by maintaining the index or distance between the burrs.

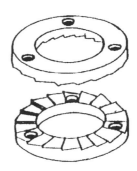

C

café filtre   Brewing method developed in France using porcelain or metal filters to brew drip coffee without electricity. The cone-shaped filter is filled with ground coffee and suspended over a mug. Water is seeped through the filter into the mug.

Caffè Latte   Italian term for a double serving of espresso with steamed milk. Café au lait in French, café con leche in Spanish and kaffee mit milch in German the caffé latte serving is roughly one-third espresso to two-thirds steamed milk, served in a large nine-ounce bowl-shaped cup or wide-mouthed glass. Lattes are also embellished with flavorings added before the espresso, or steamed with milk.

caffeine   An alkaloid found in the leaves and berries of coffee, chemically identical with theine (an alkaloid found in the tea plant); used as a stimulant and diuretic. Espresso coffee has less caffeine because arabica beans are used (less than half the caffeine of robusta beans) and usually roasted longer (darker), which further reduces the caffeine content.

cappuccino Usually equal thirds of espresso, steamed milk, and frothed milk served in a five-ounce cappuccino cup. Steamed milk at the bottom of the frothing pitcher is poured over the espresso, and the froth at the top of the pitcher is spooned on top to "cap" the cappuccino and retain heat. Cappuccino is often garnished with a light sprinkle of chocolate or cocoa, cinnamon, nutmeg, vanilla powder or color sugar crystals.

Capuchin An Italian religious order of monks distinguished by their brown hooded robes, said to have discovered cappuccino as a recipe using "coffea arabica" with milk in a drink that helped keep them awake during prayer sessions. The color of their drink matched the color or their robes.

carafe Glass vessel used for pouring water into the machine and to collect the coffee during the brewing cycle. The carafe has a lid and handle assembly, and level markings that show water and coffee capacities.

coffee basket(s) Also called filter sieves or brew baskets, the coffee baskets are usually stainless steel in one- and two-cup sizes. The bottom of the coffee basket has small perforations that filter water through the espresso grind, restricting the ground coffee from passing through the coffee basket. Care should be taken to insure the coffee basket perforations are not clogged with coffee residue, which can restrict the flow of water through the filter holder.

colloid A gelatin-like liquid measure with very fine suspended particles that result in a very slow rate of sedimentation. The oils in a fine espresso grind form colloids that develop the golden crema encrusting the top of a properly brewed espresso serving. Overextracting espresso releases bitter oils that break down the colloids and dissipate the crema.

combination machine An espresso/ cappuccino machine with a built-in automatic drip coffee maker. The drip coffee system operates independently or simultaneously with the espresso/ cappuccino functions.

crema Often referred to as foam ("schiuma" in Italian), crema is unique to espresso. It is visual evidence that espresso has been brewed properly. Crema is the foamy, golden brown extraction that develops in the filter holder and encrusts the top of an espresso serving. It is visible, smooth and creamy, with a fresh, bittersweet taste not found in other types of coffee. The Italians claim a true crema should hold the granules of a teaspoon of sugar on top of the espresso serving before the sugar slowly descends to the bottom of the cup.

D

decaf decaffeination Technically, at least 97% of the caffeine must be removed from the coffee bean for the label to indicate "decaffeinated". Decaffeinated beans are more difficult to roast and the cost is slight higher due to the extra handling involved in the decaffeination process. It is a challenge to remove the caffeine from the beans and not remove the coffee flavor. Caffeine is water soluble and, by soaking the green coffee beans in water, solvents are used to separate the caffeine from the water. The water with the coffee flavor is added back to the beans with at least 97% of the caffeine removed.

decalcification decalcify Decalcifying a drip coffee maker or an espresso machine eliminates calcium deposits that collect inside that will eventually clog the brewing system. A decalcifier solution is used to break down calcium and mineral deposits and flush them from the system. Areas with very hard water will require more frequent decalcification, based on how often the machine is in use. Bottled (not distilled) or filtered water is recommended to avoid the build-up of calcium deposits.

delivery group The combination of the brew head, gasket assembly, shower disk, and filter holder together that contain the pressure and extract espresso from the ground coffee, delivering espresso into the cup.

doppio (espresso doppio) Double serving of espresso, usually three to four ounces, using the two-cup coffee basket in the filter holder for one double serving of espresso in a five-ounce cup.

dwell time The recovery time required for the thermostats to establish the functional temperature. Dwell time refers to the period of time it takes to raise the temperature from brewing up to steam, or from the steam temperature back below boiling for brewing espresso. Pump-driven espresso machines have at least two thermostats: one that controls the temperature under boiling for brewing espresso and a second that maintains the temperature well above boiling for generating steam.

E

espresso   A method of quickly extracting the heart of the coffee flavor under pressure in single servings, usually 1-1/2 ounce. Some believe the origin of the word is from the French "exprès," especially for you, while others believe the Italian "espresso," for fast is the source. Regardless of its origin, the result is a beverage served in individual portions with premium flavor known around the world as espresso. The many elements required to extract a true espresso with crema are well worth the effort.

extraction The brewing cycle in preparing espresso that can be timed (drawn for 20 seconds) or judged by the color of the coffee (developing a golden brown foam or crema) while brewing into the espresso cup(s). The extraction is critical. Overextracting allows too much water to pass through the grind, extracting bitter oils that break down the colloids and dissipate the crema.

F

filter Paper or mesh goldtone filters fit inside the filter basket of drip coffee makers and allow the water to filter through the ground coffee keeping sedimentation out of the cup. Paper filters are disposable and mesh filters are permanent. Be sure to use the right size filter for the filter basket.

filter basket The vessel that holds ground coffee filter in a filter drip coffee maker suspended over the carafe. Cone-shaped filter baskets improve the saturation of the coffee in the brewing cycle.

filter holder The portable handle that holds a filter and fits into the brew head, where water is dispensed through the ground coffee into the filter holder. Also called the "porta-filter", the filter holder brewing basket accepts the coffee filter basket that holds the ground coffee. Two spigots direct the flow of espresso into one cup centered under the spigots, or into two cups side by side beneath each spigot.

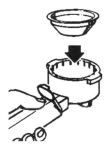

filtration A charcoal water filter system that eliminates most of the chlorine, chemicals, bacteria and other impurities from normal tap water. The use of filtered water is recommended for pump-driven espresso machines.

French roast Not the origin of the beans, French roast is a degree of dark roast. On the West Coast of the United States, some consider a French roast to be the darkest, while on the East Coast some consider an Italian roast to be the darkest roast. French roasted beans can range from light dark brown with a shiny surface to almost black with an oily surface, depending how the beans were roasted.

froth Aerated milk with a foamy texture that has been aerated or "frothed" in a frothing pitcher for cappuccino. Steam from the steam arm aerates the milk and creates small, tight bubbles that form the froth. Scalding or overheating milk will ruin the froth, much like a fallen soufflé. The froth forms a "cap" on top of a cappuccino serving to retain the heat of the espresso and steamed milk beneath the froth.

G

grinder The machine that grinds coffee beans in a variety of ways. Blade grinders, handheld mills and burr grinders are available for home use.

Blade grinders work well for coarse to medium grinds for drip coffee, stove-top and electric non-pump espresso machines, but the whirling blades offer no control over the consistency of the grind.

With pump-driven espresso equipment, the uniformity and fineness of the grind are critical and a burr grinder is recommended. Burr grinders are adjustable from a coarse grind (burrs farther apart) to a very fine grind (burrs closer together). The burrs control the consistency of the grind by maintaining the index or distance between the burrs.

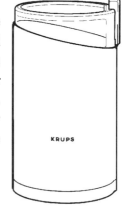

KRUPS

grounds tray A two-bin receptacle with a center bar for striking the filter holder and releasing the spent espresso pellet from the coffee basket. Also called a "knock" or "dump" box, the grounds tray can be convenient for clean-up, since espresso tends to be a very messy business. Also, if the coffee basket falls out of the filter holder when knocking out the used grounds, the coffee basket will land in the grounds tray and not the garbage, when the discovery is often too late.

H

hazelnut A hard-shelled nut from the hazel tree (birch family), also called a filbert, very popular in North America as a coffee flavoring in powder or syrup form.

heating element An electrical device used to heat water in an espresso machine, usually controlled by thermostats to maintain one temperature for brewing and a higher temperature for generating steam.

The heating element in a boiler system (non-pump or pump-driven) is located inside the boiler. In a pump-driven Thermo-Block system, the heating element is molded into the thermal block, similar to the calrod heating element of an electric stove.

hopper The container located on top of most burr grinders that holds whole beans, usually tapered to feed the beans into the grinding mechanism. Whole beans should not be stored in the bean hopper.

hull (husk) the parchment and silver skin surrounding each of two seeds inside the red coffee cherry. The two seeds inside the hull are the coffee beans. Hulling machines remove the parchment and silver skin to reveal two coffee beans from each red berry.

I

Italian roast A degree of roast, not the origin of the coffee bean. Some consider an Italian roast to be darker than a French roast, and others consider a French roast the darkest. Italian roast is often associated with espresso, but the blend and roast are a matter of personal taste.

J

Java An Indonesian island southeast of Sumatra where a type of coffee is grown. Java is now also recognized slang for coffee.

K

Kaldi The Ethiopian goat herder said to have discovered the benefits of coffee when he saw how lively his goats became after eating berries from a special tree.

Kona A district on the southwest side of the island of Hawaii that grows the best of Hawaiian coffee.

L

latte Italian word for milk and caffè latte for coffee with milk. Lattes served in North America are usually one-third espresso to two-thirds steamed milk, sometimes topped with a layer of froth, and also served here with flavored syrups. If you order just a "latte" in Italy, you will be served a glass of milk.

latteccino A recent innovation for a milk-based espresso beverage combining the consistency of a caffè latte (steamed milk) and cappuccino (steamed with equal part frothed milk). A latteccino can be considered a frothier latte or a milkier cappuccino.

lungo A "long pull" in Italian, allowing more water to flow through the ground espresso but still not overextracting the brew. An espresso lungo is roughly a two-ounce serving and should still have crema on top.

M

macchiato Espresso Macchiato is a single serving of espresso "marked" with one or two tablespoons of frothed milk. A Latte Macchiato is a single serving of espresso poured into a glass of steamed milk to "mark" the milk with espresso.

Mexicana Usually Kahlua flavor added to drip coffee or milk-based espresso drinks with heavy cream.

milk Frothed and/or steamed milk are used in preparing espresso-based drinks such as cappuccino and caffè latte. Cold, fresh milk is important to improve the frothing process, and the fat content of the milk can also affect the froth. Non-fat or 2% milk is easier to froth, but whole milk will develop a froth with more body. Half-and-half and cream will steam but will not develop a real froth because of the high butter fat content. Non-dairy alternatives, such as soy milk, are available for those allergic to milk.

mocha A chocolate-flavored cappuccino drink with roughly 1/3 espresso brewed into 1/3 frothed milk where 1/3 cocoa has been dissolved. Other variations with chocolate include adding egg white or vanilla, mocha latte with all steamed milk, a dry mocha with only frothed milk, and flavored syrups added to the mocha for a variety of signature drinks.

N

Neapolitan A stove-top brewer originating in France but adopted by the Italians in Naples. Water is heated in one chamber and inverted or flipped over a coffee chamber. Water seeps through the coffee into a serving chamber that is disconnected from the coffee chamber for serving.

nozzle The piece fitted to the end of the steam arm where steam or hot water are released through the steam arm. The nozzle has small holes or a slit that pressurizes the steam for frothing and steaming milk for cappuccino and lattes. The steam nozzle should be aerated and kept clean, since hardened milk can collect inside the nozzle and reduce the flow of steam through the steam arm.

O

oils The essence of espresso flavor is in the delicate oils of the coffee bean. The roasting process forces moisture out of the bean and brings the volatile oils closer to the surface of the bean. The darker the roast, the longer the bean was roasted, and a dark roast has a shinier (oily) surface. Very oily beans tend to stick together in the grinder and may gum up the grinder burrs and bean hopper, especially if very oily beans are refrigerated. The darker the roast, the longer the bean was roasted, and a dark roast has a shinier (oily) surface.

organic coffee Organic beans are certified by U.S. government or independent agencies to be cultivated in areas free of pesticides and chemicals in the soil used to improve a coffee yield.

overextraction Allowing too much water to flow through a one- or two-cup coffee basket, overextracting the espresso and releasing some of the bitter oils. Overextracting ruins the flavor and dissipates the crema.

P

peaberry A single round bean, instead of two flat beans, per coffee cherry. Most red coffee berries container two seeds with flat sides facing each other. These are the coffee beans. But occasionally nature provides a single round bean per cherry, called a peaberry.

Perfect Froth Patented by Krups, the "Perfect Froth" attachment on the steam arm has a rubber tip and air vent that induces more air into the milk when frothing to aerate and increase the volume of milk in the frothing pitcher.

porta-filter The portable handle and receptacle that fits into the brew head for brewing espresso in single or double servings. Usually the porta-filter holds a one-cup or two-cup coffee basket, and some have a spring-loaded grip to hold the coffee basket in place. See Filter Holder

priming Also called ventilating, priming flushes fresh water through the espresso system to prime the pump, pre-heat the brew head and filter holder, and eliminate any air pockets that may be in the system. Priming the system is key to proper maintenance of an espresso machine. Priming through the brew head flushes the shower disk of coffee residue, and priming through the steam arm evacuates any milk that may be drawn up into the arm when steaming.

psi Pounds-per-square-inch used to measure pump pressure, used in conjunction with atmospheres (ATM) and barometric pressure (BAR). One atm or bar equals roughly 14.69 psi of pump pressure.

pump Home espresso machines use a reciprocal (pulsing) or in-line solenoid pump. Depending on its size, the pump delivers between 9 and 17 bar (or 135 to 250 psi) of pump pressure. Pumps are also rated by wattage, and the average home espresso machine pump is 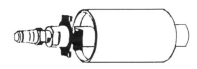 from 50 to 70 watts. The pump is vital to provide the necessary pressure to quickly force the water through a fine grind and extract the true espresso flavor with crema. Commercial equipment uses a centrifugal pump, which is a larger pump with higher capacities for moving larger volume of water under constant pressure. A centrifugal pump in a commercial espresso machine delivers a constant 9 bar of pump pressure.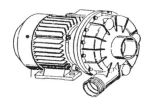

pyrolysis A critical point in the roasting process when the beans are removed from the roaster. Pyrolysis indicates a chemical change inside the beans when the surface darkens and oils develop that determine the degree of roast.

The roasting process forces moisture from the bean, and the heat makes the bean expand and lose its weight. Coffee beans are roasted at over 400°F, and the roastmaster determines at what critical point the desired degree of roast is attained.

R

ready light   Also called status lights, as the name implies the ready light signals when the water in the boiler or Thermo-Block has reached the correct temperature for brewing espresso or generating steam. Some ready lights signal "ready" when the light goes on (usually a green light) and other machines signal "ready" when the light goes out (usually a red light). The ready light may cycle on and off in the coffee or steam mode, which indicates the thermostat is maintaining the correct temperature.

ristretto   A short or "restricted" espresso where the flow of water through the brew head is stopped at about one ounce. Ristretto macchiato is a short espresso "marked" with a teaspoon of frothed milk.

roast   The process that forces moisture out of the green coffee bean and brings volatile oils closer to the surface of the bean. The darker the roast, the longer the bean was roasted, and a dark roast can have less caffeine than a lighter roast. The heat in a mechanical roaster can reach 450°F and the roastmaster controls the degree of roast by adjusting the length of time the beans are roasted.

robusta   A coffee bean species from the Congo region of Africa, called Coffea canephora. Robusta are beans grown at a lower elevation than arabica beans, cultivated for the heartiness of the tree. Robusta is lower in price and has double the caffeine of arabica beans.

S

shower disk   A perforated disk at the bottom of the brew head that channels the pressurized water to "shower" the compressed grind and totally saturate the ground espresso. It is important that the shower disk be kept clean since the perforations can become clogged with a gummy residue that will restrict the even saturation of the espresso. Refer to "Periodic Brew Head Cleaning" for instructions on cleaning the shower disk.

status lights Indicate the status of the thermostats in either the coffee brewing mode or steam mode. See Ready Lights.

steam arm Also called the steam vent or steam wand, the steam arm provides the outlet for steam generated in the boiler or Thermo-Block to flow into the frothing pitcher. Always aerate the steam arm after frothing or steaming to evacuate milk that may have been drawn into the steam arm, and wipe the steam arm with a wet cloth before the milk coating hardens.

stove-tops Non-electric espresso makers that use a gas or electric stove as the heat source for brewing coffee. The Neapolitan and Moka machines are stove-top espresso makers that produce a strong drip coffee.

T

tamper A hand held plastic device that fits inside the coffee basket to compress the ground espresso into a level bed and provide resistance by restricting the flow of water through the espresso grind. Some espresso machines feature a built-in tamper. The tamp can be critical; it can correct a grind that is too coarse, but it can also create a complete block in the brew head if the grind is too fine. A slight twist to the tamp will polish off the level of espresso grind and results in a perfect espresso with crema.

Fish

Food Town
West Washington & N. J

temperature Pump-driven espresso machines control tem thermostatically to keep the brewing temperature below boili 192°F to 197°F) and the temperature for generating steam above (from 250°F to 270°F). Because espresso is brewed in indiv servings, in order to retain heat the brew head, filter holder and espr cup should be pre-heated. Steamed milk should not reach the scald temperature of 150°F or the froth will dissipate and the milk will hav a burnt taste.

thermal carafe Insulated carafe that keeps beverages hot for up to five hours.

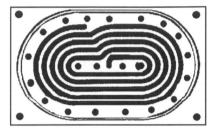

Thermo-Block A radiator-like device with a heating element in thin coiled channels that flash heat water. The Thermo-Block replaces the boiler in some home espresso machines. The separate temperatures for brewing and steaming are controlled thermostatically within the Thermo-Block. Water is pumped from the water reservoir and pulsed through the Thermo-Block where it is flash heated for brewing espresso (under boiling) or generating steam (above boiling). Steam generation is continuous in a Thermo-Block system as long as there is water in the water reservoir for the pump to draw from.

thermostats An electrical device designed to maintain the water temperature at precise brewing and steaming levels. Some machines feature a third thermostat as a safety cut-off that shuts down the machine in the event the ccomponents overheat beyond the thermostatic setting. Espresso machine thermostats are rated in either Fahrenheit or Centigrade. Electric non-pump steam pressure espresso machines have one thermostat that maintains the temperature above 200°F.

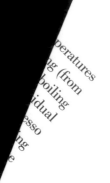

"nely ground powder-like
"atedly in a small pot
's served in small
.ds are consumed
.vily sweetened with
Because of the gritty
.fee is an acquired taste still
.ddle East, North Africa and
.rope.

underextraction The use of a grind that is not tamped properly, too coarse, or not fresh will allow water to pass through the coffee quickly and not saturate the grind to extract the true espresso flavor. An underextracted espresso is watery, weak and without crema.

V

vanilla A flavoring extract from the bean pods of tropical tall climbing orchids. Vanillin is a colorless crystalline compound extracted from vanilla beans, also made synthetically. Vanilla in syrup or powder form is a popular flavoring for drip coffee, cappuccino, lattes and steamers.

varietal Straight coffees in the green bean stage, before roasting and blending.

W

water Coffee is 98% water, and the quality of water used will directly affect the flavor of any brewed coffee. If the water is heavily chlorinated or very hard, you may wish to consider using filtered or bottled water (not distilled water). The use of bottled water also prevents the harmful build-up of calcium deposits in the brewing system. Over a period of time a build-up of calcium will reduce the power of the machine and can cause damage. Brewing equipment should be decalcified periodically, depending on the type of water and how often the machine is used.

water chamber The chamber that holds fresh water for brewing filter drip coffee.

water reservoir The reservoir that holds fresh water drawn into the espresso system by the pump. Water reservoir capacities vary from 24 ounces to more than one gallon. Some machines feature a gravity feed system and others use a siphon hose that is either built-in or drops into the water reservoir. The reservoir should never be allowed to run dry which can damage the pump. Do not confuse the water reservoir with the boiler in a pump-driven boiler system. Even though there may be water in the reservoir, the boiler may be empty and should be refilled by priming the system.

wattage Brewing equipment wattage reflects the electrical consumption required to operate the machine. The wattage on filter drip and espresso machines varies from 750 to 1500 watts. It is important that the electrical circuit used to operate the machine is not overloaded with other appliances in order for optimum performance from the machine.

The heating element and pump are two factors that contribute to total machine wattage consumption. A larger heating element in the boiler or Thermo-Block will use more electricity, and the pump is 50 to 70 watts. Grinders consume from 100 to 150 watts. Drip coffee makers range in wattage from 850 to 1100 watts.

Y

Yemen   A kingdom of the Southwest Arabian peninsula, Yemen joined the United Arab States in 1958. Supposedly, the Coffea arabica coffee species traveled across the Red Sea to Yemen during the Ethiopian invasion of Southern Arabia in 515 A.D.

Z

Zaire   Formerly the Belgian Congo region of Africa, the Coffea canephora (robusta)species of coffee was first discovered growing wild in Zaire.

zester   Handheld gadget that cuts the rind of citrus fruits in spirals for garnishing coffee beverages.